OUR NATIONAL DEBT

OUR
NATIONAL
DEBT

Its history and its meaning today

The Committee on Public Debt Policy N.Y.

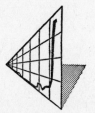

HARCOURT, BRACE AND COMPANY, INC.

CONTENTS

LIST OF DIAGRAMS

LIST OF TABLES

FOREWORD

EARLY in 1946 this Committee was organized under a grant by the Falk Foundation to make a study of policy for the management of the huge national debt. The Committee published its findings over a period of two years in seven pamphlets dealing with various phases of this question.

The writers primarily responsible for the preparation of the several pamphlets were as follows: *Our National Debt After Great Wars*, Leonard P. Ayres; *The Debt and the Budget*, Dr. Benjamin U. Ratchford; *The Debt and the Banks*, Dr. Roy L. Reierson; *The Debt and Interest Rates*, Dr. James J. O'Leary; *The Debt and Our Savings*, Mrs. Eleanor S. Bagley, Research Associate at The Mutual Life Insurance Company of New York, Stephen M. Foster, and Dr. O'Leary; *The Debt and Life Insurance*, Sherwin C. Badger, and *The Debt and the National Welfare*, W. Randolph Burgess and George B. Roberts.

While each of these studies bore the name of a different author, the method of the study was unusual in that the whole Committee took responsibility for the conclusions. Agreements were reached after extended discussions of the studies at different stages of preparation, and the resolving of differences of opinion, sometimes but not often by compromise.

This book puts these seven studies together. Considerable editing was necessary to bring early studies of the series up to date, to avoid duplication, and to tighten up the presentation. For this editing we are especially indebted to Messrs. John W. Love, Samuel T. Williamson, and George B. Roberts. The undersigned rather than the full Committee takes responsibility for the final editing.

The graphic work is by Presentation, Inc., Washington, D. C. The production and distribution of the pamphlets were directed by A. L. E. Crouter, New York Life Insurance Company, and Clifford B. Reeves, Mutual Life Insurance Company.

While the work was in progress the Committee lost five members—Brig. Gen. Leonard P. Ayres (U.S.A. ret.), Vice President of the Cleveland Trust Co., who was the author of the first report, by death; A. L. M. Wiggins, President of the Bank of Hartsville, Hartsville, N. Y., Lewis W. Douglas, President of the Mutual Life Insurance Co., and Robert L. Garner, Financial Vice President, General Foods Corp., through resignation, to accept important public offices; and Professor Harold M. Groves through resignation. These men all made valuable contributions to these studies.

Professor Wesley C. Mitchell and Stephen M. Foster died after the completion of the final chapter.

This study was made possible by funds granted by the Maurice and Laura Falk Foundation of Pittsburgh. The Foundation, however, is not the author, publisher, or proprietor of the study and is not to be understood, by virtue of its grant, as assuming responsibility for any statement or view expressed herein.

W. RANDOLPH BURGESS

January 17, 1949

INTRODUCTION

A PUBLIC DEBT which reached a high point of close to 279 billion dollars has posed a new and baffling problem to the people of the United States. Public opinion about it is not yet clarified or confident.

There are indeed some who have persuaded themselves that the debt does not matter. Others, through thoughtlessness, pay no heed to the debt and go on advocating and voting for huge government spending programs without restraint. Fortunately, this does not appear to be the typical attitude of the American citizen, who is seriously concerned about the debt; for he knows that such a huge debt will in one way or another affect the lives of every man and woman in the country, and will continue to do so for many years to come. It will influence business and employment, the incomes people receive, their cost of living, and what their savings will be worth.

In this final report the Committee sets forth five basic steps which in its opinion are essential to successful management of the debt. This five-point program for action is as follows:

1. Control the budget.
2. Reduce the debt.
3. Distribute the debt more widely.
4. Restore flexible interest rates.
5. Nourish a dynamic economy.

There is nothing novel in this program, nor anything easy and popular. There is no secret formula. The need is for nothing more or less than a stiff dose of sound American common sense.

Effective action has been made more difficult by world events since these studies were begun. Then we were thinking and talking about "One World." Today this vision has vanished. The threat of war is still with us and we are making huge expenditures for armament and for economic aid to other countries.

Another adverse development has been price inflation. The great volume of money created for war purposes has affected the economy, as was feared, in the old familiar pattern of inflation.

As against these unfavorable events, there is a brighter side. First, out of an inflated national income we have made a beginning at reducing the debt. It has been drawn down from 279 billions to 252 billions. Part of this was simply using accumulated balances to pay off debt. But the rest of it has been the solid excess of government receipts over expenditures.

Again we can take satisfaction that the country's economy has come through the first postwar adjustment with far better production and employment than was expected. Our industrial machine turned promptly from war to peacetime output and has raised our standard of living to new heights. In addition, we have fed other countries from our surplus.

All of this is evidence to support the conclusion of the Committee that this country has the power, if wisely used, to meet its foreign and domestic obligations and at the same time master the debt. The American people have time and again shown their ability and willingness to overcome difficulties if they understand what has to be done. These studies are offered to aid that understanding.

OUR NATIONAL DEBT

1

OUR NATIONAL DEBT AFTER GREAT WARS

FIVE times in our history, war expenditures built up huge public debts. Each time many thoughtful people believed that the debts were so big that we never could pay them or even greatly reduce them. This did not prove true in the four wars prior to the past one, and a review of our previous war debts may show what lessons from earlier experiences may be useful now.

INFLATION AND DEFLATION

One outstanding economic fact is that each great war produced serious inflation of commodity prices. Each time, the cost of living soared. The experience was painful; still more painful was the deflation which always followed and brought distress to farmers and unemployment to wage-earners.

The facts of war-caused inflations and deflations were recognized by John Adams, second President of the United States, who wrote: "I am old enough to remember the war of 1745 and its end, the war of 1755 and its close, the war of 1775 and its termination, the war of 1812 and its pacification. Every one of these wars has been followed by general distress, embarrassments of commerce, destruction of manufactures, and a fall in the prices of produce and of lands."

3

Diagram 1 shows the annual averages of wholesale prices from 1770 through 1948. It is striking that the Revolution, the War of 1812, the Civil War and World War I produced such huge increases of commodity prices in a brief few months, and such long drawn-out decreases with dire economic toll. Will prices in this era follow the same pattern, down as well as up? By the middle of 1948 the price level reached the peaks of previous great wars. Many believed that artificial government control of prices would have saved us from the inflation which followed other wars. Whether or not it could have done so, most controls were suspended in the autumn of 1946.

In the War of 1812 and the Civil War, prices broke almost immediately when the fighting stopped. But after World War I, prices rose for eighteen months after the armistice. More than three years after the end of World War II, prices were still high, though there were indications that the end of the rise might already have occurred.

It is worth noting that the depression following the War of 1812 forced wholesale prices far below those when war inflation got under way. This was partly because even before we went to war, the country was affected by price increases of the Napoleonic wars. After the Civil War, a fairly continuous deflation carried prices down to levels almost identical with those when inflation began. In the 1880's and 1890's prices fell still lower, but the Civil War's deflation probably should be considered ended when gold payments were resumed in 1879. World War I inflation began in 1914 with prices at 99 (in terms of an average 1910-1914 equals 100 per cent) and carried them to 226, but the subsequent two-

---

Sources of data used in diagram on facing page. The index is that compiled by Professors Warren and Pearson for the period 1770 to 1890 with variable group weights. The all-commodity index of the Bureau of Labor Statistics is used from 1890. Average 1910 to 1914 is taken as equal to 100.

DIAGRAM I

WHOLESALE PRICES made great increases in war periods followed by declines long drawn out.

Average 1910-14 = 100

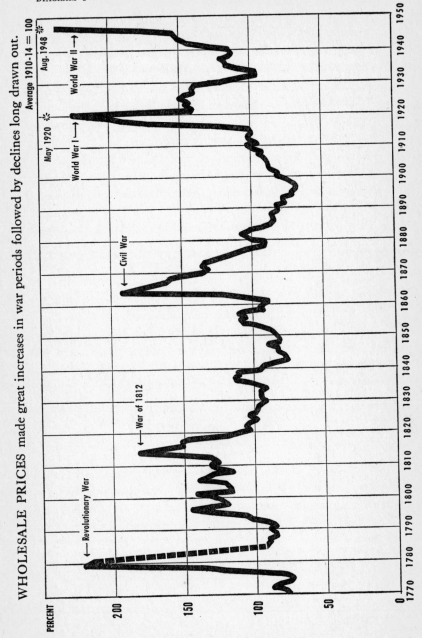

OUR NATIONAL DEBT

stage deflation brought 1932 prices virtually back to the 1914 level. Despite the similarity of some of these movements, we should look into causes and not assume that the statistical pattern will be repeated. Nevertheless, it is interesting that wholesale prices during and after World War II rose in much the same manner as in World War I.

INFLATION AND THE DEBT

One of the few economic findings about which there is fairly widespread agreement is that wartime price inflations are caused by governments having to spend more than they can raise in taxes. They either print or borrow the money and pour into the hands of the people more than they have normal ways of spending. There is also a scarcity of goods— and thus the now-familiar spectacle of lavish spending from swollen pocketbooks.

In theory, excessive price rises could be avoided by taxing the people so heavily that the Government could regain all the extra money it paid in war wages and contracts. No government has ever found how to do this. One reason is that the new money is unevenly distributed, and heavy taxes might fall on people who have received none of it. Another reason is that taxes must be voted by politicians likely to lose their jobs if tax policies are too bold.

In our country's early wars, there was no adequate or elastic tax machinery. In the Revolution, the central government had no taxing power whatever and levied on the states with pathetically poor results. Toward the end of the war, for example, Robert Morris persuaded Alexander Hamilton to become a tax collector in New York in the hope that with his great and rising influence he might persuade New York State to raise and pay to the government her assessment for the year 1782 of $365,000. In spite of his most vigorous efforts Hamilton collected only $6,250, and before many months resigned the position as hopeless. In this situation, with no banks from which to borrow and with France and Holland making only modest loans, the Continental Congress resorted perforce to the printing of paper money which eventually was "not worth a continental."

National government was more firmly established by the time of the War of 1812. But neither Congress nor the Treasury was ready with a financial policy adequate for the extraordinary demands of armed conflict. Three times—in 1807, in 1808, and again in 1810—Secretary of the Treasury Gallatin proposed that should war come, it should be financed by loans, and that taxes should be increased only to cover expenses of the peacetime establishment and interest on new loans and existing debts. He even declared that in no event would he insist on internal taxes. Thus developed the doctrine of war financing associated with his name, a doctrine which the historian Hildreth referred to in these caustic words: "Out of a tenderness for the people or a tender regard for their own popularity, Congress had resolved to carry on the war without imposition of taxes."

Fortunately, the increase in expenditures was relatively much less than during later wars. About 57 per cent of total costs of the War of 1812 were met by borrowing and about 43 from taxes and other receipts.

For financing the Civil War, Congress was extremely slow in increasing taxes. In the first year of the war 90 per cent of the expenditures were met by borrowing and 85 per cent in the second year. For the war as a whole, borrowing accounted for 77 per cent of the expenditures, and 23 per cent came from taxes and sale of land.

This country entered World War I with two new features in its tax structure which enormously aided war financing. One was the income tax on individuals and corporations.

The other was the excess profits tax on corporations. These were made legal in 1913 by the Sixteenth Amendment to the Constitution. Despite these new features, taxation met only 28 per cent of the war's expenditures; borrowing was 72 per cent. One reason was that World War I outlays were ten times those of the Civil War.

World War II's expenditures were ten times those of World War I, yet 46 per cent of the needed funds came from taxation, 54 per cent from borrowing. This record was achieved by vigorous use of income and excise taxes.

The discouraging part of the picture is that even with drastic application of a modernized tax system, more than half our costs were still raised by borrowing—by the very method which has proved to be inflationary. This raises the uncomfortable question whether our spending was unnecessarily lavish. Of course, penuriousness never won a war, and Americans do not resent the huge outlay for the atomic bomb, but we pay the cost in rising living expenses and later deflations. We need to be alert in time of war, and especially at the end of each war, to limit unneeded and costly bureaus and functions.

THE CHANGING PER CAPITA DEBT

In 1790, when Alexander Hamilton, then 33 and the first Secretary of the Treasury, had been in office only a few months, he estimated the new nation's public debt at about 72.4 million dollars. The foreign debt which was owed mostly in France and Holland was 11.7 millions. The domestic national debt was 42.4 millions of which one-third was arrears of interest. And debt to the states for services and supplies amounted to 18.3 millions.

These sums seem small today but were embarrassingly large then. To the young nation, short of capital and impov-

DIAGRAM 2

PER CAPITA NATIONAL DEBT of World War II broke into wholly new ground.

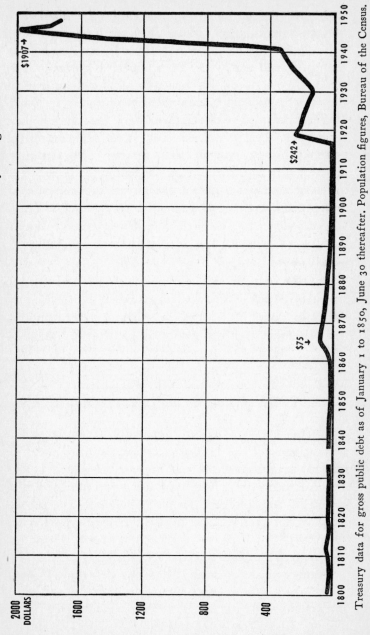

Treasury data for gross public debt as of January 1 to 1850, June 30 thereafter. Population figures, Bureau of the Census.

erished by war and inflation, 72.4 millions in hard money was enormous. The debt had to be borne by a population of only 3.9 millions, mostly poor farmers, traders and frontiersmen. Moreover, when Hamilton entered the Treasury, confidence in the Government's ability to pay was so low that certificates of public indebtedness sold at 10 and 20 cents on the dollar.

Diagram 2 records changes in the national debt from Hamilton's time to the present. It is per capita—the figures for the total debt in each year are divided by the population of the country—and it shows the burden of the debt which rested on each man, woman and child. In 1790, the debt could have been wiped out if each inhabitant of the United States paid in $19 to the national Treasury. After the War of 1812, each person would have had to pay $15. After the Civil War, the figure rose to $78; and after World War I it was $240. In 1948, after the debt had been reduced somewhat, each one of us would have had to pay about $1720 to extinguish the debt—this over and above tax collections each year to keep the Government running.

DEBT AND THE NATIONAL INCOME

Perhaps a better way to appreciate the size of the national debt is to compare it with the net yearly income before taxes of the total population. Diagram 3 shows that comparison. The earliest estimate that we have of national income is for 1799, as compiled by the National Industrial Conference

Sources of data used in diagram on facing page. Data for national income are those of the National Industrial Conference Board from 1799-1928, and the income payments series of the Department of Commerce from 1929 to 1948. Conference Board figures prior to 1900 were available only at 10-year intervals. Intervening data were computed by means of data on business fluctuations. National debt is gross debt from *Statistical Abstract*.

DIAGRAM 3

NATIONAL DEBT AS PERCENT OF NATIONAL INCOME was below 60% until World War II and then rose to over 150%.

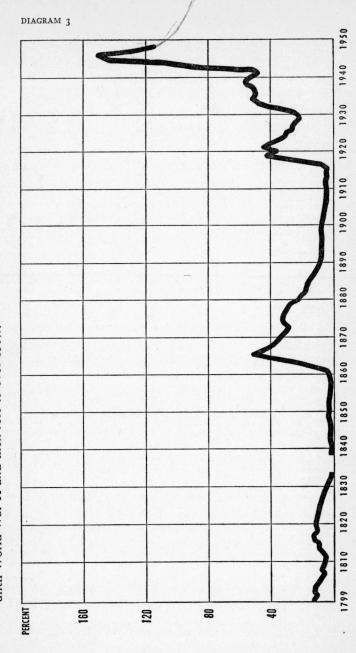

Board. At that time the public debt was about 78 million dollars and was 11.6 per cent as large as the national income. It therefore may be fairly inferred that when the new Federal Government was organized, its public debt was a little less than 10 per cent of one year's national income.

The first Secretary of the Treasury resigned in 1795 mainly because he could not support his large family on his $3,500 salary. Although his successor was an able man, federal finances were less skillfully handled. Not until 1807 was the national debt reduced below that when Hamilton took office. When the War of 1812 broke out, the debt was down to 45.2 millions and a little more than 5 per cent of national income; then it rose rapidly until in 1816 it was over 129 millions and about 13 per cent as much as national income.

Serious inflation then developed, money deteriorated and government securities sold below par. For loans of over 80 millions the Treasury received only 34 millions as measured in specie, and once it increased its debt by five millions to borrow less than one million. Its securities sold for the ridiculously low price equivalent of $19.

After the War of 1812, the country grew rapidly. Income from customs and sale of public lands was high, and government receipts were greater than expenses. Public debt was steadily reduced. By 1835 it was entirely paid off, and in a spirit of optimism the Treasury's surplus was distributed among the states. Symptoms of the coming panic and great depression of 1837 were already developing but were not recognized, as indeed such symptoms seldom are. The Mexican War in the middle forties caused no considerable rise in the public debt, nor was there any until the outbreak of the Civil War in 1861.

By the war's end in 1865, the debt had grown to 2,675 million dollars, and was 50.2 per cent of national income. But only one-ninth of the debt was in obligations of more than two years' specified maturity. A contemporary critic thus described the debt: "Eight-ninths of it consisted of transient forms issued under laws made up to a great extent of incomprehensible verbiage giving unlimited direction over the mass to one man, and expressing in the aggregate nearly 100 contingencies of duration, option, conversion, extension, renewal, etc."

We never did pay off the Civil War debt entirely, but we pared it down steadily for 28 years until it was only 839 millions, or about one-third of what it was at its peak. In 1893 it was about 7 per cent as large as that year's national income. It rose to 1,282 millions by the time we entered World War I, but the country's wealth had increased faster, and the debt was only 3 per cent of national income. Although by 1919 it was up to about 41 per cent, it was less of a burden than the Civil War debt.

By 1930, after steady down payments, the 16-billion debt was 22 per cent of national income. Deficit financing lifted this figure in 1931 and a decade later came the great burst of World War II expenditures. By 1945, the debt was 142 per cent of the income of the American people for that year. At the peak in February, 1946, it was 160 per cent, or a total of 279,214 million dollars. Our present war debt is therefore different from all earlier ones.

IS THIS DEBT MANAGEABLE?

Here, then, is a debt of unprecedented size, incurred in fighting an unprecedented war. It is another evidence of the disrupting influence of total war, in which the whole of a country's energies become engaged. The purpose of this study is to seek ways of measuring the weight on this country of the huge war debt, and its probable effects; and to explore

methods by which it can be handled with the least damage
to our national economy.

This involves a whole series of questions, such as: By what
methods and how rapidly can the debt be paid off? How
heavy taxes ought we all to bear to pay off the debt, remembering, of course, the effect of taxes in impeding both personal
and business operations? Who should hold the bonds which
represent the debt—banks, insurance companies, private individuals, or others? How can its inflationary effects be reduced
and alleviated?

One of the immediate questions the debt provokes is the
amount of interest which must be paid each year to the holders of the debt, that is—the people and institutions from
whom the Government has borrowed the money. Since the
end of the war the Government has been paying more than
five billion dollars a year. This item alone is more than total
peacetime governmental expenditures for all purposes in any
year before 1931. We should examine this huge interest payment carefully and critically.

INTEREST AS PER CENT OF NATIONAL INCOME

Just as we do not consider the debt solely in dollar terms
but in relation to other factors affecting our capacity to pay,
so we should compare this interest figure with the national
income out of which it must be met. Diagram 4 shows what
percentage of our national income is represented by interest
payments on our national debt from 1799 to 1948. The proportion was 0.8 per cent shortly after the War of 1812 and
about 2.6 in the Civil War. Just after World War I, the
percentage rose to nearly 2.0 and was not much less in the
great depression years of 1932 and 1933. Shortly after the
end of World War II it rose to 2.8, the highest in our history.

DIAGRAM 4

INTEREST ON THE DEBT as percent of national income, while greatly increased by World War II, is now below Civil War peak.

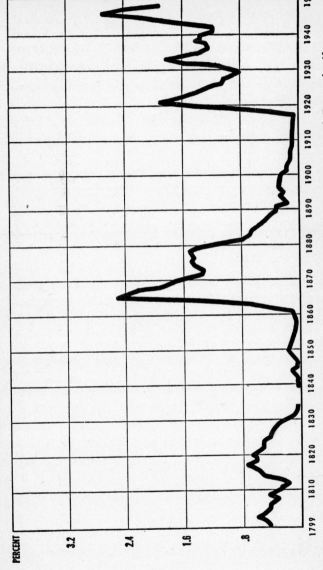

Data to 1860, computed for each issue; later data from *Statistical Abstract*, 1926, and *Economic Almanac*, 1946.

A subsequent marked rise in national income caused this percentage to recede somewhat.

In a sense, this is the first encouraging evidence yielded
by examination of the national debt. Despite a debt 100 times
the size of the Civil War debt and ten times that of World
War I, interest payments, in proportion to national income,
are now actually below the Civil War peak.

While this is true, the improvement in the ratio of interest
to national income means that inflation has been getting in its
work. To be sure, a high national income makes it easier to
collect taxes, but to the extent that it is due to mere marking
up of prices, it reflects the gravest danger of the debt—dilution of the dollar, which is discussed in a later chapter.

Present national income is over 220 billion dollars, as compared with 57 billions just after World War I. This rise is due
both to higher prices and to a great increase in production and
distribution of goods. Nobody knows whether and how long
this expanded income will last. Should it shrink, interest on
the debt would be harder to pay because taxes would be
harder to collect. Another reason why the interest burden is
no heavier is that interest rates are the lowest ever experienced in this or any other country.

INTEREST RATES ON NATIONAL DEBT

Diagram 5, next page, shows the interest percentage on
our national debt from 1790 to 1948. The rates shown for the
first four decades are lower than the actual prevailing rates
at that time because part of the newly funded debt paid only
3 per cent and all interest on another part was deferred until
1801. War with Mexico stiffened rates in the late 1840's, and
they moved up to record highs in the Civil War.

From that war to World War I, the course of interest on
the national debt was mostly downward. Public credit was

DIAGRAM 5

INTEREST RATE ON INTEREST-BEARING NATIONAL DEBT moved to a record high level in Civil War, to a record low in World War II.

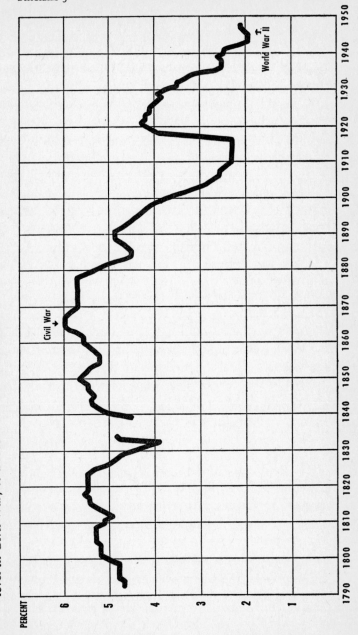

strengthened largely by the Government's demonstrated ability to pay off its large debt. It was influenced by the enhanced value of government bonds, some of which had the circulation privilege of national bank notes. Interest rates rose sharply during and shortly after World War I and have declined most of the time since then. From 1943 to 1946, the average rate was 2 per cent or less. This was the first time we ever incurred a great war debt without material increase of interest rates.

It is indeed extraordinary that when its need for money was greatest, the Government could borrow at the lowest rates in all its history. One reason was monetary management. All the facilities of the Treasury and the Federal Reserve System were used to keep interest rates for borrowing low. Other chapters will describe how this was done and the advantages and disadvantages; the point to be noted in this historical account is the great change from when a weak national government was forced to pay 8 per cent interest to induce the public to lend it money, to a time when the Government can in a measure dictate the rates at which it sells its bonds to the public.

Over this length of years, confidence in the United States Government has strengthened, the country's wealth has grown, its taxing system has developed; but even more important has been the increased governmental control over money. The chief reason this became possible was establishment of the Federal Reserve System in 1914. Through its operation, the Government can change the amount of money in the banks and even in the hands of the public.

In exercising such powers to keep money rates low in World War II and after, the United States was not alone. Other governments the world over did the same thing. By their controls, they circumvented the normal wartime tendency for laws of supply and demand to bring higher interest rates. One result is a large interest saving to the Government; but there are others. While keeping rates low, the Federal Reserve System had to pump money out into the spending stream and thus create inflation at the source. There is a question whether at these lower rates the Treasury could sell as many bonds to investors—and keep them sold—as it could have at higher rates; also whether the amounts taken by banks and the Federal Reserve System have not been larger than necessary.

SELLING BONDS TO THE PEOPLE

Control over the interest rate by monetary management was aided by new development in another side of debt financing: a vigorous sales program for widespread popular purchase of bonds.

During the Civil War, Jay Cooke taught the federal authorities that appeal to patriotism would greatly help their financing, that quantities of war bonds could be readily sold to individuals as well as to banks. These lessons were closely followed in World War I financing. Liberty Loan bonds were made convenient for the individual investor by being issued in denominations down to $50, and in either coupon or registered form, with the various types interchangeable. Early issues were tax exempt, except for estates and inheritances. The country was organized through the Federal Reserve System for a vast bond-selling campaign. Millions of citizens became bondholders for the first time and so associated themselves with the war effort.

Perhaps the most serious criticism of management of the World War I debt is that appeals to patriotism, and resort to social pressure, were employed so effectively that the Treasury Department sold its bonds at prices which were probably higher than their current investment values. Nearly all new issues sold below par throughout the war despite the fact that they progressively carried higher coupons. When interest rates stiffened further in 1919 and 1920, bond prices dropped and caused much dissatisfaction among many patriotic but inexperienced investors. For example, the second 4¼ per cent Liberty Bonds callable in 1927 sold on the New York Stock Exchange in May, 1920, at $81.10, a price which yielded more than 7½ per cent to call date.

In World War II, the Treasury profited from both the successes and mistakes of World War I. It followed the program of vigorous, widespread sales, and, in the hope of avoiding declines in market values of securities held by small investors, it put out obligations adapted to different groups of purchasers. Nearly one-quarter of the added debt has been in non-negotiable savings bonds and savings notes which are not subject to price quotations on security exchanges. This largely removed the danger that numbers of small holders might sell on falling markets as did owners of World War I Liberty Bonds. With this type of security and by energetic sales campaigns, over 75 million people purchased bonds.

There has been a noteworthy evolution of war financing philosophy. American fiscal authorities have swung all the way from belief that most or all the new debt should be sold to banks, to the conviction that as little as possible should be lodged in banks. Widespread ownership of the debt is not only a vast aid in financing a war but in the long run should give the people a wholesome interest in sound governmental fiscal policy.

LESSONS OF HISTORY

From this survey of the record of the debt in past wars, certain lessons should help us to deal wisely with this great problem today. These experiences, and their application to the task of debt management before us, may be summarized as follows:

1. Five times in this Nation's history we have incurred great national debts—always to finance wars. Each time government war spending and borrowing have given us price inflation, followed in each case up to the present by painful deflation.

2. The inflationary forces in World War II have been greater than ever before, accompanying wholly unprecedented increases in war spending and government debt, both in dollars and in relation to population and national income.

3. Though interest on the debt amounts to over five billion dollars a year, its proportion to national income is about the same as after the Civil War. This is partly because of the much greater national income, and partly because of a governmentally-imposed low interest rate policy, which has other serious economic implications.

4. It has been our national tradition to pay down our war debts promptly, and increasing national wealth always enabled us to do so.

5. Throughout our history, the greatest obstacles to national strength and the most acute dangers of fiscal collapse have been weak financial policies, but never inadequate or failing resources. During the 157 years from 1792 through 1948, we have had ninety-five years of net surplus in our national budget and sixty-two years of net deficit. That record is good enough to encourage us—and poor enough to put us on guard.

6. George Washington gave some good advice on war debts in his Farewell Address of September, 1796. He said:

"As a very important source of strength and security, cherish public credit. One method of preserving it is to use it as sparingly as possible; avoiding occasions of expense by cultivating peace, but remembering also that timely disbursements to prepare for danger frequently prevent much greater disbursements to repel it; avoiding likewise the accumulation of debt, not only by shunning occasions of expense, but by vigorous exertions in time of peace to discharge the debts which unavoidable wars may have occasioned, not ungenerously throwing upon posterity the burdens which we ourselves ought to bear."

Data used in preparing the material in this chapter have been taken largely from U. S. Treasury Reports and the following books: Davis R. Dewey, *Financial History of the United States*; Rafael A. Bayley, *National Loans of the United States from July 4, 1770 to June 30, 1880*; William F. DeKnight, *History of the Currency of the Country and of the Loans of the United States to 1900*; Robert A. Love, *Federal Financing*.

2

THE DEBT AND THE BUDGET

MANAGEMENT of the national debt depends on the Nation's annual budget. When we spend more than we raise in taxes, the budget deficit creates more debt. Without a budget surplus debt cannot be retired.

During the war, our 100-billion dollar budget reflected the enormous, insistent demands of total war, regardless of economic consequences. Our fiscal policy was confined to ways and means of raising these vast sums in such manner as would least disturb war production and would minimize the inflationary effects of federal spending.

THE NUMBER ONE PROBLEM OF FEDERAL SPENDING

When the war ended our first task was to re-establish control over spending. Otherwise, all talk of debt "policy" was idle. We had to decide what constituted a reasonable budget. And that decision depending not only on what we wanted government to do, but also upon our willingness and ability to foot the tax bill without stifling enterprise and slowing up production.

So that the reader may see the upward march of government expenditures Diagram 6 on page 24 and Table 10 in the Appendix are presented showing over-all budget totals from 1914 to 1950. Here is a full panorama of the rise and fall of government spending during and after two world wars. World War I expenditures rose from less than one billion dollars in 1914 to 18.5 billions in the fiscal year 1919. After that expenditures fell rapidly. Three years later they were under 3.4 billions, about one-sixth of the wartime

DIAGRAM 6

U. S. GOVERNMENT EXPENDITURES over 40 billions, though contracted since the wartime peak, are still more than four times pre-war.

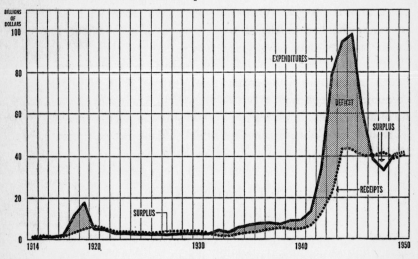

peak and close to the annual average for the years 1922-30.

In the 1930's, expenditures rose largely because of depression spending for relief and pump-priming. They were influenced by increasing public acceptance of the spending philosophy and of government responsibility for social welfare. By 1939 expenditures were at a new peacetime record of nine billions, or about three times the general level of the twenties.

Then came rearmament, followed by war. Annual expenditures soared to the dizzy peak close to 100 billions. From this they fell to a postwar low of 34 billions in the fiscal year ending in June, 1948. They have since risen to an estimated 40 billions in 1949 and 42 billions in 1950. These figures, given in the latest budget, do not take account of the transfer directed by Congress of three billions of foreign Economic Cooperation Administration expenditures charged to fiscal '48, but actually made in fiscal '49.

Although this is a big decline from wartime, it is still enormous. Three years after World War I the budget was reduced five-sixths from its wartime peak. In three years since World War II the reduction was less than two-thirds. In the fourth year of peace, our Government spends in one year more than it did during all of World War I and more than four times as much as in 1939, the peacetime high up to then. As for the fifth year beginning in July, 1949, a still greater outlay is contemplated. As disclosed by President Truman in January, 1949, expenditures for defense and other items approach those of the first calendar year of the war.

WHERE THE MONEY GOES

The question naturally arises, where is all this money going? Table 1 and Diagram 7 (pages 27 and 26) give the breakdown of the 42 billion dollar spending proposed for the fiscal year 1950, compared with figures for 1939. Classifications are the same as used in the budget.

Four items alone total 31.9 billion dollars, over three-fourths of the whole budget. They are national defense, veterans' services and benefits, interest on the public debt and international affairs and finance. These are staggering increases but another disturbing feature is the mounting expenditures under almost every heading. Aside from the "Big Four" items, the expansion of all but two of the major pro-

DIAGRAM 7

WHERE THE MONEY GOES. Comparison of 1939 and 1950 budgets shows large increases for most major programs.

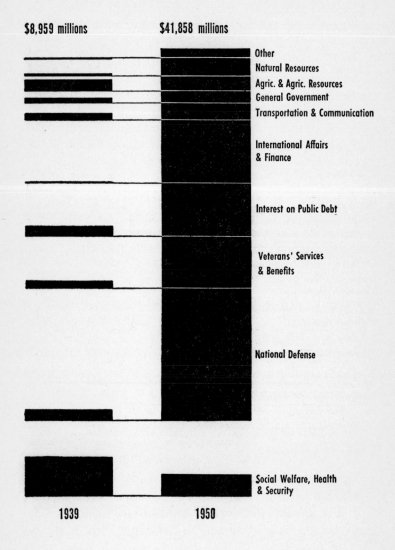

$8,959 millions $41,858 millions

Other
Natural Resources
Agric. & Agric. Resources
General Government
Transportation & Communication

International Affairs & Finance

Interest on Public Debt

Veterans' Services & Benefits

National Defense

Social Welfare, Health & Security

1939   1950

gram classifications is from 100 to more than 1,000 per cent. One of the exceptions is "social welfare, health and security." Expenditures for work relief and direct relief practically disappeared during the war. But for this decrease, expenditures under the social welfare heading would have been more than double those of 1939. Total expenditures under the latter item are exclusive of appropriations for old-age insurance financed by social security taxes and handled through government trust funds.

TABLE I

BUDGET EXPENDITURES BY MAJOR PROGRAMS

(Amounts in millions)

	1939	1950	% Change
National defense	$1,074	$14,268	....
Veterans' services and benefits	559	5,496	+883.2
Interest on the public debt	941	5,450	+479.2
International affairs and finance	19	6,709	....
Social welfare, health and security	3,996	2,358	− 41.0
Transportation and communication	512	1,586	+209.8
General government	556	1,224	+120.1
Agriculture and agricultural resources	1,198	1,662	+ 38.7
Natural resources	214	1,861	+769.6
Housing and community facilities	154 *	388	
Finance, commerce, and industry	52	107	+105.8
Labor	11	187	....
Education and general research	44	414	+840.9
Reserve for contingencies	....	150	
Adjustment to daily statement basis	63 *		
TOTAL EXPENDITURES	$8,959	$41,858	+367.2

* Excess of credits, deduct.

Three factors help to explain this rise in government expenditure:

1. The number and scope of functions we expect government to undertake. War and its aftermath left such vast

obligations as national defense, veterans' pensions and benefits, interest on the public debt and international economic
aid. Belief prevails widely that government should be responsible for managing the economy and protecting the individual. There is continued political pressure to enlarge government operations in countless directions—to grant subsidies
and guarantees to various population groups and to promote
many new welfare activities, all of which involve larger and
larger appropriations.

2. Governmental inefficiency. The past fifteen years have
been ones of lavish spending. Money has come easy to the
Government. Prudent management has been discouraged by a
philosophy that government spending is a virtue in itself.
Wartime spending habits are hard to break. Under such conditions, waste and inefficiency unavoidably creep in.

3. The price level. Under the higher level of prices, wages
and salaries, it costs the Government proportionately more
to supply the same services it furnished in 1939.

WHY WORRY ABOUT GOVERNMENT SPENDING?

The question may be asked, does not government spending mean more purchasing power in the hands of the people,
more employment and business activity and more national
income out of which to pay taxes? Will it not in large measure pay for itself? Why worry?

There are three reasons for concern. *First,* high government spending makes debt management more difficult. It
makes it not only harder to achieve a budget surplus needed
to pay off debt, but there is always danger that a moderate
decrease in revenue would make budgetary deficits unavoidable and actually increase the debt.

Second, big government spending impedes tax reduction,
and all taxes have a more or less repressive influence on

economic activity. Under heavy spending, it is harder also to avoid bad taxes. When demand for funds is great, legislators are more likely to turn to taxes which may be expedient politically though unsound economically. Temptation is strong to settle with an eye to those with the most votes.

Third, the mere effort of putting billions of dollars annually through the Government's financial machinery is expensive. It includes the cost of levying and collecting taxes, checking tax returns, trying tax cases and making disbursements—to say nothing of the time-consuming efforts of taxpayers to comply with complicated tax laws. Regardless of other effects. these operations are a "drag" on the economy.

EFFORTS TO CUT GOVERNMENT COSTS

The President expressed growing concern in August, 1946, over the trend of government expenditures: "The present inflationary situation makes it imperative that expenditures be cut to the minimum compatible with the responsibilities of government." Still the budget remains too big. It is true that outlays for defense and for European recovery have had to be increased, but the budget calls for putting about 20 per cent of the greatly expanded national income through the Federal Government. Even with revenues estimated at around 40 billion dollars in fiscal 1949 and 1950, the President forecasts a small deficit for both years. With the announcement of the executive budget for fiscal 1950, responsibility now shifts to Congress. Certain tentative conclusions may be drawn:

1. The present governmental structure has over 1,800 separate bureaus, services, and units, a four-fold increase in the last twenty years. It is now so vast and complex that the organization itself is out of control, and the whole mechanism cries out for streamlining. Vigorous, continuing effort

will be needed to bring government spending down to reasonable size.

2. Great savings can be made by reducing excess personnel, eliminating duplication and enforcing greater administrative efficiency. Economies will require, however, careful discrimination to avoid impairing essential services, particularly those which have neither dramatic public appeal nor any lobby to support them.

3. Major savings are impossible without reconsideration of broad policies for which Congress is largely responsible. For example, consider our huge military expenditures. What savings can be made through more efficiency? Is our national defense adjusted to new scientific methods of warfare, or are we spending for obsolete weapons, equipment and training? Is our military policy consistent with our foreign policies? Are the different branches of the service co-ordinated to that policy?

Another policy in need of re-examination is the timing of public works and projects for development of natural resources, transportation and communication. While inflation remains a menace, these projects should be deferred to a time when outlays for them would help economic stability rather than increase inflationary pressure.

4. Cutting the budget is a political as well as an economic problem. Success depends on public opinion. Every budget cut hurts or inconveniences some person or some group, and a fight is put up against that particular retrenchment. An effective long-term program of government efficiency and reduction of unnecessary costs requires public education and support of sound policies.

Reduction of government costs is not an easy nor a simple problem. It cannot be solved quickly. It calls for continued, vigorous effort and a united determination by the administration, Congress and the people to bring our Government to a higher measure of efficiency. Thus it may serve the people more adequately and at the same time will not be so expensive as to interfere with the country's economic well-being and retard its dynamic growth.

RATE OF DEBT RETIREMENT

Control of spending is the most immediate requisite of debt management. A longer-range problem is what should be done about paying off the debt.

As we have seen, it is in the American tradition to pay down our war debts promptly. Discussions in Congress, in the press and elsewhere make clear that the American people want to reduce the World War II debt. It was reflected in the 64 to 20 vote in the Senate, March 3, 1947, to pay out of budget surplus at least 2.6 billion dollars on the national debt in the fiscal year 1948, a goal which was much exceeded.

The burden of heavy interest is not the only consideration. A later chapter shows how increased debt greatly expands the money supply—always dangerous at a time of inflationary psychology. The size of the debt and its service reduces the freedom of action of the Treasury and the Federal Reserve System in their credit policy. They are limited, for instance, in taking restrictive credit action which would raise interest rates.

The debt's size heightens the danger to the country of wrong policies; it is one thing to make mistakes in handling a small debt, but far more serious and costly when the debt is great. The heavier the debt and current interest load, the harder it would be for government to finance readily and wisely some future emergency, such as another war or depression. The American tradition of paying down debt is based on sound reasons.

Almost everyone agrees that the time to reduce debt is

when business is active, employment is up and national income is high. People have money then to pay taxes. Treasury revenues are expanded, and government expenditures for relief are, or should be, low. Then, too, debt retirement in prosperous times acts as a brake upon over-expansion and inflation.

By both these tests, we must continue to reduce the debt. But how much and how fast? That depends partly upon who holds the debt.

THE QUESTION OF DEBT OWNERSHIP

When a budgetary surplus is used to redeem securities held by the banks, that payment reduces bank deposits and the money supply—provided, of course, that banks don't expand credit in other ways. This deflationary effect is multiplied when Federal Reserve banks hold the retired debt; it reduces reserves of commercial banks and encourages further credit contraction. In recent months, such a policy of restraint has been desirable, though it might not be so at other times.

Payments out of budgetary surplus do not account for all bank-held public debt that is retired or transferred. A further reduction takes place more or less automatically through the workings of our social security laws and the sale of savings bonds to investors. Under the Government's accounting set-up, social security trust funds are built up outside the regular budget—from taxes levied on employers and employees and interest collected on investments. This money, which is accumulating at about three billion dollars a year, buys "special" issues of government securities and thus becomes available to the Treasury for retirement of public marketable debt, including that held by the banks. Also available for such debt retirement are funds received by the Treasury from

sales of savings bonds which in calendar 1948 exceeded re-
demptions by 2.2 billion dollars.

Diagram 8, which charts investor group holdings of the
debt to the end of September, 1948, shows that commercial
banks have had the largest reduction in dollar totals. Securi-

DIAGRAM 8

DEBT HOLDINGS BY INVESTOR CLASSES show principal
reductions have been in commercial bank holdings.

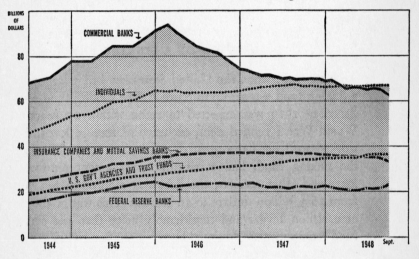

ties held by corporations—not shown in the diagram—likewise declined, though much less. Insurance companies and
mutual savings banks have reduced their government obligations by more than three billion dollars since the peak. On
the other hand, holdings by individuals and government trust
funds continued to grow.

The 19-billion reduction in commercial bank-held debt
during the last ten months of 1946 was from excess Treasury
balances built up by the Victory Loan, the last of the war loan
series. Inasmuch as these cash balances were held inactively

on deposit in the banks, their cancellation, together with a corresponding amount of debt, was not actually deflationary. It merely removed an inflation potential. Retirement or transfer of bank-held debt in other ways, however, has had a deflationary influence.

During calendar 1947 and the first nine months of 1948 this latter influence operated to the extent of about 12 billion dollars, largely through the retirement of bank-held debt from surplus revenues, social security trust fund accumulations, and sales of savings bonds.

THE QUESTION OF A SINKING FUND

In the past, when the United States has had a large debt, a sinking fund was set up to retire it. The sinking fund established in 1919 was expected to retire within 25 years the World War I funded debt, exclusive of foreign loans. This worked well until the great depression of 1929. Thanks to the sinking fund, budget surpluses, repayment on foreign loans and other receipts, the debt was reduced in ten years from 26½ billion dollars to 16 billions. This was at the rate of a billion a year and considerably more than the sinking fund requirement. Additional borrowings after 1930 increased the public debt, but for several years the Treasury continued to go through the bookkeeping motions of operating the sinking fund. Eventually, sinking fund purchases were reduced and since 1944 have been discontinued, but annual appropriations are still made for this purpose and the unexpended balance is allowed to accumulate.

To wipe out the present debt in fifty years, we would have to pay annually five billion dollars on principal; to pay it off in 100 years would require 2½ billions a year. The fifty-year program would entail a total of interest and principal payment of 10 billion dollars a year at the outset, slowly tapering down as interest costs diminished. The 100-year program which the U. S. Senate favored in 1947 would mean annual principal and interest payments of about 7½ billions during early years. These are fairly Spartan proposals, but the 100-year program calls for about as little retirement as is prudent in normal years.

Another proposal is more flexible. It would firmly limit government expenditures in normal and boom years. It would require a tax system which would develop moderate surpluses in fairly prosperous years and large surpluses in boom years, these to be used to cut the debt. On the other hand, in depression years, the retirement would be less and in a severe depression the debt might even be increased.

This broad purpose would be served by a sinking fund geared to the national income. For example, suppose a few years hence a national income of 200 billion dollars would be a reasonable average of good and bad years. Suppose further that a reasonable sinking fund payment in a normal year should be 1½ per cent of the national income, or three billions. Then, as the national income increased, the sinking fund could be a larger percentage. Conversely, a lower percentage would apply as national income fell. This plan would be definite yet varied enough to meet changing economic conditions.

Any of these plans is better than none. Congress should set a policy. A formal sinking fund of some kind would remind Congress of the necessity of providing for debt reduction and it might have some influence for limitation of expenditures in normal years. It would be an orderly, systematic method of debt reduction, and particularly desirable when political bodies are tempted to find new ways of spending and to postpone debt payment until some more "convenient" time.

A PRACTICAL GOAL IN DEBT RETIREMENT

Under any of the foregoing programs, how much debt retirement should be anticipated? Barring another emergency, how large should the federal debt be thirty or forty years hence?

The "proper" size of the debt depends on various factors such as whether we are increasing or decreasing it and how well the financial system is adjusted to it. For instance, during the last five or six years, it was possible, even desirable, for us to maintain a debt considerably larger than would have been feasible under 1941 conditions. The price level is much higher, financial habits of individuals and business firms have changed and government bonds bulk large in the portfolios of banks, insurance companies and trust funds. These cannot be altered drastically and quickly without serious consequences, and, as far as we can see now, it is not likely that they will return to their pre-war status.

Debt reduction is accomplished at a price. The price and the advantages to be realized vary with the amount of debt to be retired and with economic conditions. The price includes the burden of tax collection, what deflationary pressure comes from debt reduction, and the effects of shifting portfolios. The advantages are lowered interest charges, less likelihood of inflation, and a decrease of all danger inherent in a big debt. Today, the price for retiring the first layer—say 30 or 40 billion dollars—is so low contrasted with advantages that unquestionably the deal is a bargain. But as we go beyond that in the next decade the price is likely to go up while advantages decline.

It is impossible to say where price and benefits will balance. We ultimately retired about 65 per cent of the total Civil War debt and about 40 per cent of World War I debt.

The important point is that we need not plan now to retire the whole debt. It will be enough if we set as a goal an annual amount feasible in relation to the national income. There is time enough later to reset our sights, if the goal then seems too high or too low.

TAXES, THE DEBT, AND ENTERPRISE

Taxes, the third major element in the budget, are the means for meeting expenditures and reducing debt. In the face of rising government costs and the necessity for debt reduction, revenue must be large and continuous. This means taxes should have a broad base not solely for their yield but because the more taxpayers there are, the greater should be popular support for economical and efficient government.

Tax reductions always have a strong popular appeal, while debt reduction arouses, at most, only mild public enthusiasm. But tax reduction should not be too fast. It should not cut off revenues needed for debt retirement. Moreover, it is far easier to reduce than increase taxes; not for a century has the United States levied a new tax or raised the rates of an old one to finance debt reduction.

THE TAX DILEMMA

Tax reductions should be governed by prevailing business and financial conditions. When there is a shortage of goods and labor, when prices are rising, when profits are high and speculation is prevalent, there is a good case for high tax rates and for devoting all available surpluses to debt retirement. Such a policy would have double benefit—reduce debt and ease inflationary pressure. Yet, taxes are always a repressive burden on the economy. If we are to bear the weight of our public debt without discouragement and stagnation, dynamic growth is essential—and that is a major reason for reducing taxes as soon as possible.

One way nations have managed their war debts is summed up in the phrase, "growing up to the debt." Our own Civil War debt looked huge at the time. Many regarded Britain's debt increase prior to and during the Napoleonic wars as threatening the future of that country. Actually, neither debt was an insurmountable obstacle. We paid down our Civil War debt; Britain followed the course of not reducing greatly the amount of the debt but of letting the growth of the country reduce the burden relatively. The debt programs of both countries was immeasurably helped by the rapid growth of national wealth and income during the Nineteenth Century.

Our debt management would be simpler if we could look forward to a continuance of this country's long-term growth. Regarding that possibility, Professor Sumner H. Slichter of Harvard said in 1946:

> "One consequence of the dynamic character of our economy is the rapid rise in output. Back in 1890 the net national production for the entire year was about as much as we turn out now every forty days. For ten or fifteen years after the war we shall probably see a rapid rise in the national production, even though we put only a small part of our annual production into increasing capital. . . . By 1960, we should have a gross national production of comfortably over $300,-000,000,000—in terms of present prices. This year [1946] our national production gross will be in the neighborhood of $190,000,000,000. Hence there will be a rise by 1960 of over 50 per cent.
>
> "It is not always easy to visualize these future increases in production. It is easy to get into the habit

of doing all of one's thinking in terms of present magnitudes—a very dangerous habit."

Such increases in production might occur in any of a myriad directions, but the obvious sources of funds for more debt service and retirement would be industries which have grown rapidly since the war. Among these are electric power, petroleum, chemical and farm machinery industries. The possibilities in atomic power lie in the future, and so do a number of developments nearer at hand, like the gas turbine, but the recent surge of television suggests what may happen when conditions are ripe for growth. It takes little imagination to see how improvements in transportation, communication and agriculture enable people to earn more money and thus carry a great debt more easily.

To reach the levels of production envisioned by Professor Slichter, people must have incentive to strive and take risks. That incentive is seriously impaired by a tax system which penalizes rather than encourages those who contribute most to material progress.

RESTRICTIVE EFFECT OF TAXES

How our federal tax bill has grown during recent years is shown by Diagram 6. Since 1939, when taxes were already high, total net collections increased from 5.1 billion dollars a year to an estimated 41 billions in 1950. Direct taxes on corporations, exclusive of employment and excise taxes, rose from 1.3 billion to 12.3 billions, while direct taxes on individuals, with the same exceptions, increased from 1.4 billion to 20 billions.

Corporate income tax rates doubled, from 19 per cent to 38 per cent. In 1939, the individual normal tax rate was 4 per cent, after personal exemption of $2,500 (for a married couple with no dependents) and after an earned income credit, while the surtax started at 4 per cent on $6,500 and rose by degrees to 75 per cent on income over $5,000,000. Today net income over a $1,200 exemption is subject to combined normal tax and surtax, starting at 16.6 per cent and rising to 82 per cent on everything over $400,000.

As far down the income scale as $1,500 a married couple find an extra dollar of earnings worth only 83 cents to them after they have settled with the tax collector. From there on up the income scale their incentive to strive to make the extra dollar is rapidly and progressively diminished. At $10,000 the worth of the extra dollar has shrunk to 81 cents; at $25,000 it has become 67 cents; and at $50,000 it is down to 51 cents. At $100,000 they can keep only 37 cents of the extra dollar, and financial incentive for extra effort and extra risk is close to the vanishing point. For the unmarried taxpayer, who does not have the advantage of splitting income for tax purposes under the joint return permitted in all states under the Federal Revenue Act of 1948, the rates of course are much higher.

The question to be considered in any long-range program is the effect upon the growth of the country, and our ability to carry our enormous war debt, of a tax scale that exacts such heavy and increasing penalties upon those who make the extra effort, take the extra risk, and assume the extra responsibility. The objective is to encourage the long-range planning that will carry established industries forward, start new businesses, and enable small businesses to grow. Most small businesses are in the form of individual proprietorships and partnerships and hence are taxed at the high individual rates.

This then is the tax problem—to maintain a revenue system that will yield the large sums required by our still huge budget, yet will leave room for a flourishing economy under which the debt burden may be carried more easily. We shall return to this subject in the final chapter.

THE "COMPENSATORY" BUDGET

Of all proposals for budget and debt management, the most controversial is the "compensatory" budget. According to this school of thought, government should engage in "compensatory" spending to make up any deficiency in private spending. Some form of deficit financing would have to pay for it, and among various schemes proposed are issue of paper money and interest-free borrowing from the banks. Some plans suggest tax reductions or refunds during depressions; but most plans rely on acceleration of government spending, financed by sales of government securities to the banks which would inflate bank credit and expand the money supply. Periods of expansion would call for a reversal of government spending. Taxes, according to this theory, would be increased, expenditures curtailed, and the money supply would be reduced by applying budget surpluses to retirement of bank-held government debt.

Some go so far as to advocate a continually rising debt as a measure to avert economic stagnation. This assumes that our economy, as now organized, will be chronically short of enough consumer purchasing power to take off the market all the goods or to pay for all of the services which a full and efficient employment can produce. More extended discussion is given in Chapter 5. Enough here to say that the proposed remedy has not worked convincingly enough to justify risking the financial stability of the Nation to adopt it.

The compensatory plan rests upon the extremely naïve and superficial theory that all ills of our economy can be cured by the use of more and ever more money. A clogged fuel line is not always the cause of a stalled motor car. Perhaps the carburetor is flooded; if so, there's no point in pouring in more gasoline. Were we to accept the spending hypothesis and it proved unsound, we would be so deeply committed that we might not be able to withdraw without disastrous consequences.

FOUR GREAT OBSTACLES

Even if the compensatory budget theory was flawless, there would still be four formidable obstacles to successful operation. The first is that of practical administration. Our federal fiscal machinery is far too cumbersome and rigid for execution of elaborate policies requiring accurate timing and precise co-ordination. According to Professor Charles C. Abbott of Harvard University, "the more ambitious goals of many current fiscal-policy doctrines are beyond the capabilities of the existing mechanisms of public financial administration, and for the most part are far removed from the purposes for which such mechanisms were created." [1]

The second hurdle is political. As pointed out by Dr. Roy Blough, former director of tax research in the Treasury Department, Congress does not act with the speed and precision which a workable compensatory policy requires. Nor is it likely to delegate the necessary powers to any administrative agency. From his specially favorable vantage point, Dr. Blough comments on the "flexible" tax system:

> "The problem is to get legislative bodies and the taxpaying public to move with such agility as to keep abreast of the necessary changes. The designation of a small group to make the adjustment would be a very helpful step. . . . There is at present little prospect,

[1] Charles C. Abbott, *"Administration of Fiscal Policy,"* Harvard Business Review, Autumn, 1944, p. 62.

however, that Congress would grant to any administrative agency, or even to a committee of its own ap-
pointment, the power to operate a flexible system of
taxes. . . . For Congress itself to operate on the flexible basis would involve serious problems of getting
Congressional attention and understanding as well as
the time lag during consideration of the proposal. . . .

"It should be observed, moreover, that a substantial
lag in the measures taken under a flexible tax program
might be more harmful than no effort to use such a
program, since the result of delay might be that the
intended measure would be put into effect at just the
wrong time." [2]

The third obstacle is also political. It involves the willingness of Congress to pursue policies economically wise but
politically unpopular. Although it might not be difficult to
persuade Congress and the public to approve increased spending to counteract a depression, the real test of the compensatory program would be the resoluteness of Congress and the
people to limit spending to offset a boom. In efforts to reduce
our tremendous war-expanded budget, we see today how
hard it is to reduce government expenditures once we have
become used to spending.

The fourth hurdle is the inflationary effect of striving to
reach whatever goal compensatory spending aims at. Suppose
that the goal is maintenance of full employment—planned
spending would hardly be content with one less ambitious.
Long before that goal is reached, we know by experience,
bottlenecks occur in labor, materials and productive capacity,
and prices are forced up by sellers' markets in one commodity
after another. With full employment comes increased labor
turnover and decreased productive efficiency. A tight labor

[2] *The American Economic Review*, Supplement, June, 1944, pp. 16-21.

situation strengthens unions' bargaining position, and tends towards a wage-price spiral.

Even advocates of compensatory spending admit this weakness in their theory. One of the authors of the White Paper committing the British Government to the full employment principles is Professor John Jewkes of the University of Manchester, England. He has stated frankly that "most of the problems of maintenance of employment arise from the fact that the policy of full employment involves the danger of inflation." [3]

Sir William Beveridge, noted English economist, shares with the late Lord Keynes the distinction of having done most to promote the compensatory doctrine. He has said: "There is no inherent mechanism in our present system, which can with certainty prevent competitive sectional bargaining for wages from setting up a vicious spiral of prices under full employment." [4]

However good compensatory spending may look on paper, it has many unresolved questions both in theory and practice. At least at present, the doctrine would not be acceptable to the American people. Debt retirement is primarily a long-term basic policy, and its flexible adjustment to changing conditions cannot be relied upon as an economic instrument.

POLICY AS TO FLOATING DEBT

Related to debt retirement is the short-term or "floating" debt, and what shall be done with it. This is the public marketable debt, chiefly Treasury bills and certificates of indebt-

[3] Address entitled *"Second Thoughts on the British White Paper on Employment Policy"* before National Bureau of Economic Research, New York, June, 1946.
[4] *"Full Employment in a Free Society"* by William H. Beveridge, W. W. Norton & Co., New York, 1945, p. 199.

TABLE 2

COMPARISON OF U. S. FLOATING DEBT AND TOTAL DEBT BY TYPES OF SECURITIES, NOVEMBER 30, 1948

(Amounts in billions)

Public Marketable:

    Floating Debt

Bills	$ 12.4	
Certificates	26.0	
Notes	3.5	
Bonds	.6	
	$ 42.5	

    Over One Year

Notes	$ 3.6	
Bonds	111.6	
	$115.2	
Total Public Marketable Debt		$157.7

Non-Marketable Debt:

Savings bonds	$ 54.9	
Savings notes	4.6	
Special issues to government agencies and trust funds	31.4	
Armed forces leave bonds	0.5	
Treasury bonds, investment series	1.0	
Depositary bonds	0.3	
	$ 92.7	
Total Non-Marketable Debt		$ 92.7

Non-Interest Bearing Debt:

Special notes—International Bank and Fund	$ 1.2	
Other non-interest bearing	0.9	
	$ 2.1	
		$ 2.1
GRAND TOTAL DEBT		$252.5

edness, which matures within one year. At the end of November, 1948, it stood at 42½ billion dollars or 17 per cent of the total debt, or 27 per cent of the total marketable debt. Table 2 shows the composition of both the floating and total debt by types of securities. Diagram 9 traces the course of

DIAGRAM 9

FLOATING DEBT, while down from peak
following end of the war, is still heavy.

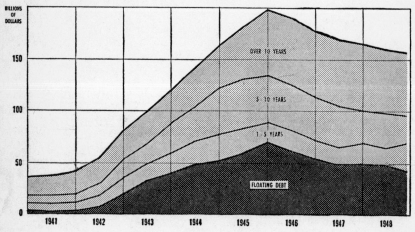

the floating debt during and after the late war, together with the trend of longer-term marketable issues.

Each succeeding year, the Treasury must refinance these floating debt securities, some of them several times a year. In addition, there are other potentially short-term obligations, including 47 billion dollars of marketable issues that will mature by 1955. Practically redeemable on demand are 59 billion dollars of non-marketable savings bonds and savings notes. Also 31 billion dollars of special issues to social security and other government trust funds and agencies are redeemable within one year or on demand. Adding these to the floating debt gives a total of 133 billion dollars in securities that mature or could be redeemed within a year. This is more than half of the total federal debt.

In a depression, many savings bonds would be cashed by the public, and some special issues would be redeemed to meet unemployment insurance payments. Otherwise, it is unlikely that large amounts of savings bonds and special issues would be presented for payment. But they are possible claims, and the Treasury must be ready to meet them, as well as handle the floating debt.

This is one reason why the floating debt should be materially reduced. There are others.

1. This debt is held predominantly by banks. Hence its reduction in a period of inflation would tend to hold down the money supply and ease inflationary pressures.

2. With a large floating debt maturing and refinanced each year, a rise in interest rate would increase debt charges rapidly. Account must be taken also of the large issues maturing within a few years which will move into the floating debt classification.

3. An excessive floating debt makes public debt operation less flexible. When the Treasury needs money quickly in an emergency, it must sell short-term issues which banks buy and pay for by expansion of bank deposits. If the floating debt is already disproportionately large, more short-term issues cannot be sold without added inflationary risk.

REDUCING THE FLOATING DEBT

There are two principal methods of reducing the floating debt. One is to pay it off out of budget surplus or other cash balances on hand. The other is by conversion into longer-term obligations.

Conversion is chiefly a problem of placement of refunding

issues. One possibility is to step up the sale of savings bonds to the public. These securities have proved their popularity, and since the war their amount outstanding has increased by more than eight billion dollars. Another refunding medium is sale of special issues to social security and other government trust funds. Although both savings bonds and special issues are redeemable at short notice, their turnover is relatively slow, and they are less sensitive than floating debt issues to changes in interest rates and other conditions.

Largely by drawing on the cash proceeds of the Victory Loan, the Treasury effected through retirement a big cut in the floating debt—from 68 billion dollars February 28, 1946, to 54 billions at the end of 1946. During the same time, Treasury sales of 600 million dollars net in savings bonds and 3½ billions in special issues to government trust accounts provided four billions for refunding short-dated debt. During calendar 1947 and 1948, a budget surplus supplemented savings bond sales and social security fund accumulations, resulting in a further reduction of the floating debt to 42½ billions. From 1949 through 1952, however, 46 billions of marketable bonds become subject to call, and all of these bonds will have reached final maturity by the end of 1955, thus indicating an accentuated problem of refunding if a renewed rise in the floating debt is to be avoided. The entire debt will mature within twenty-three years.

Still another conversion of floating debt is by additional offerings of long-term marketable Treasury bonds, ineligible for purchase by commercial banks. The main purchasers are insurance companies, savings banks, pension funds and other institutional investors. By offerings such as these when occasion warrants, the Treasury could gradually "chip off" considerable floating debt. Amounts and timing would depend on market conditions and availability of funds. Successful operation might call from time to time for higher interest than rates now prevailing, but the result is so important that modest rate increases should be made when found necessary.

These refunding operations can be a powerful aid in reduction of inflationary bank credit and in bringing the country's money supply into balance with its production of goods. They make it easier for the Treasury to handle its maturing obligations; and they give both Treasury and Federal Reserve System greater freedom of action in restraining credit expansions.

MEN AND MECHANISMS FOR DEBT MANAGEMENT

The more one explores the national debt situation, the greater is the realization that here is one more field in which responsibilities of government are enormously increased. For in the handling of this huge debt, mistakes are magnified and the need for proper management cannot be exaggerated.

Probably in no other matter of major importance do administrative officials of the Federal Government have so much discretion as in determining policies of debt management. Congress usually does no more than set a limit on the total amount of the debt and prescribe a few other general features. Most of the important decisions are made by Treasury officials with the aid of the Federal Reserve staffs. This is necessarily so, for the subject is highly technical, and market conditions often require quick changes of policy; but it means that considerable power and discretion rests in the hands of a few high administrative officials of the Treasury. It is vitally important that these men should be capable and experienced, that they have efficient and responsible staffs and that compensation, pension arrangements and recognition should be adequate to their responsibilities.

One interesting experiment in the search for better budget

control is a provision in the Legislative Reorganization Act of 1946 for a legislative budget as well as an executive one. The committees on appropriations and revenues of both Senate and House are required to consider jointly the budget proposals submitted by the President, then to recommend to Congress a legislative budget which, when accepted, is an advance commitment on over-all expenditures and amounts to be raised in taxes. This plan was expected to correlate the spending and taxing functions of Congress more effectively. Unfortunately, it is not working well, but the objective is so important that it calls for further study and effort. Congress is abdicating a fundamental duty if it fails, either through want of proper co-ordination of spending and taxing or through subservience to the executive branch, to exercise control over the public purse.

Men and mechanisms are about as important to debt management and budget control as sound policies. The size of the budget is so great that mechanisms for dealing with it should be modernized. And the responsibilities and power which management of the public debt demands, emphasize that here is one more field in which high competence in government is required.

SUMMARY

1. Both the war and prewar spending policies brought about an enormous expansion in the functions and cost of government. Because excessive spending dilutes the money supply and limits the Government's freedom in dealing with debt and taxes, regaining control of the budget is the Number One task of debt management. Such control is again threatened by new spending programs.

2. A policy of debt reduction is desirable because the size of the debt and its service (a) adds to the tax burden and

restricts the freedom of the authorities in their credit policies, (b) makes mistakes in debt management more serious, and (c) renders more formidable the problem of financing some future emergency.

3. Practically all schools of thought agree that the time to reduce debt is in periods of prosperity, and especially when inflation threatens. At the same time we must be ever mindful of the importance of a vigorous, dynamic economy in carrying the debt burden. Because high taxes are one of the greatest handicaps to enterprise we must reduce them as rapidly as we soundly can. This is partly a problem of timing in relation to business and financial conditions, and partly a problem of getting expenditures down to yield a budgetary surplus, available for both debt and tax reduction.

4. Over the long run, neither a policy of rigid, inflexible debt reduction nor a "compensatory" policy of using debt fluctuations as the chief instrument for economic stability is best. The problem is to work out a formula that will keep debt retirement moving along at a rate the country can afford and yet have some flexibility to meet changing conditions. While it is neither necessary nor wise to plan now on retiring the whole debt, we might well agree on some tentative annual program that seems reasonable in proportion to national income, and adjust later on the basis of experience.

5. A large floating debt imposes problems of refinancing, impairs flexibility in fiscal planning, and increases the danger of inflation. A substantial part of our floating debt should be paid off out of budget surpluses or funded as rapidly as markets can be found.

6. The vast growth in the functions of government makes imperative their more effective operation. This calls both for improving the mechanisms and providing conditions to hold capable people in government service.

3

THE DEBT AND THE BANKS

THE first objective in a war is to win it. Another objective is to avoid disruption of economic life, both during and after the conflict. The two objectives are partly irreconcilable; war is won at the expense of economic dislocations which leave grave problems. And gravest of all is inflation.

Basically, inflation is a problem of money, taxes and banking. To pay for a war, government takes from the people all the taxes they are believed able to pay, and sells them all the bonds they can be persuaded to buy. But that is not enough. The deficiency is met by the ability of commercial banks to extend credit. Government borrows from the banks by selling them its securities, and in payment the banks write up deposit credits for the Government to use.

This process inflates the banking system, both assets and deposits, far beyond its natural size and even changes its structure. It affects commercial and central banks profoundly and brings about new relationships between them. All this greatly involves the public interest. Inflation of the banking system inflates the money supply, permeates our whole economic structure and affects the everyday lives of all of us.

I. COMMERCIAL BANKS AND WAR FINANCE

The experience of banks in financing the First World War was elementary compared with their role in the Second.

52

History supplied no precedents. The war was "total" to an extent nations had never before attempted and to a like degree our banks and financial resources were employed in the struggle.

Banks played a big part in war loan drives. They composed the biggest single group of sellers of war bonds. Three-quarters of the dollar volume of war loan campaign sales were made through commercial banks. In addition, these institutions performed less spectacular but equally essential services. They took bond subscriptions, issued savings bonds, delivered securities, made collections on coupons and bonds and carried on countless other functions. Their help is reflected in the low financing cost to the Treasury of the small denomination savings bonds. Between May, 1941, and April, 1946, 1.1 billion individual savings bonds were sold at a financing cost of only $\frac{1}{42}$ of 1 per cent.

But the main story of the banks in the war is far more significant. That story includes an account of what the great wartime expansion of money supply did to the earnings, strength and safety of the banks. It also reveals how the banks became predominantly investing rather than lending institutions, how they were still recognizable at the war's end as banks, but not the same banks the country had known for generations.

Briefly, the World War II financing program and the commercial banks' part in it was this:

1. In the five fiscal years of war, from July 1, 1941, through June 30, 1946, the United States Government spent 370 billion dollars.

2. Of this total, 169 billions or 46 per cent came from taxes. The balance of 201 billions was met by borrowing. Although this showing does not equal what some had hoped for, it was much better than that of the World War I fiscal

DIAGRAM 10

HOW THE MONEY WAS RAISED.
(July 1, 1941 — June 30, 1946)

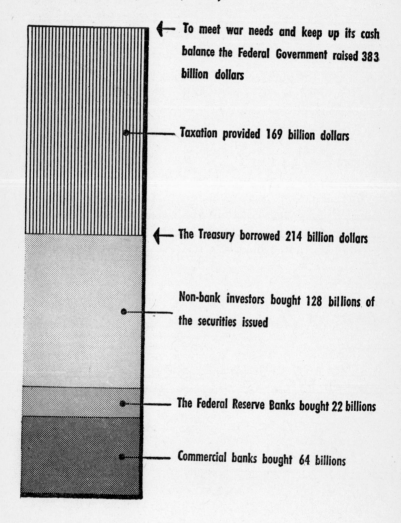

← To meet war needs and keep up its cash balance the Federal Government raised 383 billion dollars

Taxation provided 169 billion dollars

← The Treasury borrowed 214 billion dollars

Non-bank investors bought 128 billions of the securities issued

The Federal Reserve Banks bought 22 billions

Commercial banks bought 64 billions

years 1917-1919, when current revenues supplied only 28 per cent of government expenditures.

3. To meet its deficit and build up a cash working balance, the Treasury borrowed 214 billions during the five years. Of this amount, about 128 billions came from non-bank investors, some 22 billions from the Federal Reserve Banks, and the balance of 64 billions, or 30 per cent, from commercial banks. (See Diagram 10.)

4. On July 1, 1941, commercial banks held 19.7 billions of government debt. By June 30, 1946, their holdings were 83.3 billions. Despite this huge increase, the percentage of bank holdings to the total debt actually declined from 36 per cent to 31 per cent.

5. Commercial banks supplied additional funds for defense and war purposes by lending to business and by making loans which enabled others to buy government securities. Their lending operations among private borrowers increased by nine billions during the war.

TABLE 3

WARTIME CHANGES IN LOANS AND INVESTMENTS OF INSURED COMMERCIAL BANKS

(Dollar amounts in billions)

	Dec. 31, 1939	Dec. 31, 1945	Increase	
			Amount	Per Cent
Government securities	$15.6	$ 88.9	$73.3	471
Loans	16.9	25.8	8.9	53
Other securities	6.9	7.1	0.2	4
TOTAL	$39.4	$121.8	$82.4	210

EFFECT ON BANK CREDIT

Between 1940 and 1945, commercial bank investments quadrupled (see Diagram 11 and Table 3), yet their loans showed relatively small increase. Usually, bank lending operations are larger during times of greatly expanded industrial activity. Although never before was such industrial expansion as during World War II, bank loans did not keep pace. Government financed most war plant construction and

DIAGRAM 11

INVESTMENTS OF INSURED COMMERCIAL BANKS
quadrupled from 1940 through 1945 while LOANS
showed relatively little increase.

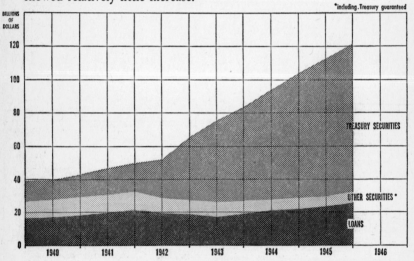

made large advances on war contracts. Between 1942 and 1946, war production loans of 10.3 billion dollars were authorized and guaranteed by such government agencies as the War and Navy Departments and the U. S. Maritime Commission.

Besides these government loans, there were additional reasons for the comparatively small increase in bank lending. Tax accruals, unspent depletion and depreciation allowances and retained earnings gave business concerns large amounts of cash and cut down their need for loans. With farm income up, agricultural loans declined, and new mortgage loans were few because building was restricted. High employment, bigger wages and the absence of such consumer goods as auto-

DIAGRAM 12

LOANS OF INSURED COMMERCIAL BANKS rose from 1940 through 1945, but most of the increase was for buying government securities in War Loan Campaigns.

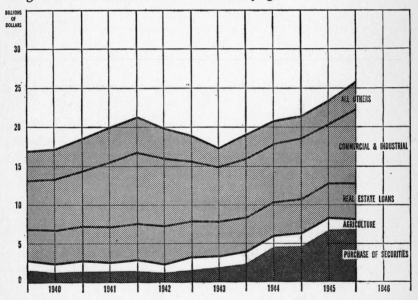

mobiles enabled many people to reduce their indebtedness.

Changes in the totals of different types of bank loans are shown in Diagram 12 and Table 4 (page 58). Almost 60 per cent of the rise in bank loans between 1940 and 1945 was for purchase of securities, mostly government obligations. Most of the remaining increase was in commercial and industrial loans. This showing is much different from that of World War I, when bank loans more than doubled and security holdings increased much less. But there was a different Treasury policy. "Borrow and Buy" was the motto of World War I financing; in World War II, this was discouraged as inflationary.

TABLE 4

WARTIME CHANGES IN LOANS OF INSURED COMMERCIAL BANKS

(Dollar amounts in billions)

	Dec. 31, 1939	Dec. 31, 1945	Increase or Decrease (—)	
			Amount	Per Cent
Commercial and industrial	$ 6.3	$ 9.5	$3.2	49
Agricultural	1.1	1.3	0.2	20
Purchase of securities	1.6	6.8	5.2	320
Real estate loans	4.1	4.7	0.6	13
Other loans	3.7	3.5	—0.2	—4
TOTAL	$16.8	$25.8	$9.0	53

HOW BANKS FITTED INTO THE TREASURY PROGRAM

It was a ticklish decision to determine how far the Treasury should rely upon the banks in financing the war. The dilemma recalls the old saying, "We can't live with 'em and we can't live without 'em." Those charged with working out the wartime financial program well knew that the war could not be financed without some expansion of bank credit; they also realized that too much of it could bring disastrous inflation.

The Treasury program aimed to hold to a minimum any increase in public buying power in the form of bank deposits and currency. This was imperative because few civilian goods were available. The wartime rise in incomes could not be allowed to exert its full inflationary influence. Consequently, as many non-bank investors as possible should buy bonds out of current incomes or idle cash.

It was also vitally important that every war loan should be over-subscribed. To fall short of the goal would have been like losing a battle and would have reflected on the Nation's morale and will for victory. In their readiness to take what could not be sold elsewhere, commercial banks were in a sense underwriters of government security issues. But if too big a proportion of funds was raised by the easy method of borrowing from banks, the accomplishment would have been hollow indeed; that way led to inflation.

Because of this, wartime banking and credit policies had a difficult dual objective. To support the financing program, commercial banks were encouraged to invest in government securities. But unrestricted bank purchases would cause the money supply to shoot up; and commercial banks were therefore limited in the issues and amount of securities they could buy.

HOW BANKS WERE ENCOURAGED TO BUY SECURITIES

Several steps were taken to enlist commercial banks in war loan campaigns and help them to buy government securities.

Step One: Banks were permitted to open deposit accounts in favor of the U. S. Treasury, and to pay for security purchases by crediting those accounts. By so doing, they could buy without putting up any money until the Government drew on its accounts. Banks were also allowed to handle customers' bond purchases the same way.

Step Two: Another inducement was removal of reserve requirements against these government (war loan) accounts. The Treasury deposits were also exempt from deposit insurance assessments. Banks were encouraged not only to subscribe to security offerings themselves but to solicit subscriptions from their depositors.

Step Three: By guaranteeing markets, the Federal Reserve System made it attractive for banks to keep fully invested without fearing that their reserves were insufficient for all contingencies. It fixed buying and selling prices on three-month Treasury bills, and this encouraged banks to invest excess funds in short-term securities yielding an annual return of ⅜ of 1 per cent free from risk. Because a bank could convert them into cash at virtually a moment's notice, these income-producing bills were equivalent to cash. Furthermore, the Federal Reserve Banks stood ready to buy one-year ⅞ per cent Treasury certificates when banks had to meet unexpected demands for funds or wished to build up reserve balances.

Step Four: A fourth encouragement to commercial banks was the Federal Reserve Banks' so-called preferential borrowing rate. Under this, banks could borrow at an interest cost of only ½ of 1 per cent a year on short-term government obligations maturing or callable within a year. Banks could thus buy ⅞ per cent one-year certificates, confident that if they needed to they could borrow against them at low cost.

Step Five: The great rise in their deposits during the war increased the amount of reserves banks were required to hold. At the same time, the rapid increase of money in public circulation—money originally obtained from banks—forced bankers to draw down their reserve balances with the Federal Reserve Banks so as to meet the needs of their customers. To relieve this scissor-like pressure, the Reserve System provided commercial banks with additional reserves, in part by reducing the percentage of reserves which banks were required by law to hold against demand deposits in New York and Chicago where pressure was severest.

Step Six: In addition, Federal Reserve Banks bought government obligations in the open market whenever it appeared that commercial banks needed reserves. From a level of some 2½ billion dollars in the middle of 1942, Federal Reserve holdings of government securities rose to some 25 billions at the end of 1945. With reserve balances available to them, it was unnecessary for banks to make substantial borrowings from the Federal Reserve during the war; and generally easy credit conditions prevailed in the money markets.

Because of the arrangements and concessions in these six steps, commercial banks attained comparatively full investment without the risk of running short of funds. They could therefore meet without strain all government needs for funds not filled from other sources.

HOW BANK PURCHASES OF BONDS WERE RESTRICTED

While commercial banks were encouraged to participate in war finance, in other respects they were restricted. As the war went on, the Treasury curtailed bank acquisitions of long-term bonds. Government bond offerings to banks generally were limited to securities maturing within ten years or less. Longer-term bonds were not made eligible for bank holding until ten years of their maturity. After the Third War Loan, direct subscriptions by banks during war loan drives were discontinued except for limited purchases against savings deposits.

The purpose of these limitations was to help keep the banking system liquid and the money market flexible and to hold down the interest rate. But it was not a simple matter to manage the banking and credit system so that banks would buy enough government securities to put a war loan campaign over the top, and at the same time avoid over-easy conditions that would encourage banks to add unnecessarily to their security holdings.

In the early years of the war, the Treasury policy worked out pretty much according to plan. Bank purchases approximated the total of unsubscribed securities offered public investors. By the end of 1944, however, it was apparent that the restraints upon bank purchases were becoming less effective than encouragements to invest. The balance had tipped toward generous credit and reserve conditions, and interest rates declined.

It is difficult to say whether lower interest rates and greater readiness on the part of banks to buy discouraged other buyers and brought about unnecessary expansion of bank credit. The evidence is not convincing. In the Victory Loan of December, 1945, there was expansion of bank loans to speculators subscribing to bonds. Otherwise, the pace of bank credit expansion for 1945 was about the same as for earlier war years. But the main question is whether there would have been less inflation of bank credit and more buying by non-bank investors had wartime money rates been higher. Again, this is debatable and cannot be decided from available evidence.

II. THE EFFECTS OF WAR FINANCING

Our World War II financing program had four major effects upon our banking system.

1. The money supply expanded greatly at a time when goods were relatively scarce.

2. The main function of commercial banks shifted from that of short-term loans to business to short, medium and long-term loans to government.

3. Capital funds of these banks did not increase as fast as their deposits.

4. Bank earnings rose substantially.

HOW THE MONEY SUPPLY INCREASED

Never before in our history had the money supply been so large either in total or in relation to national income. During the six defense and war years of 1939-1945, money in circulation almost quadrupled, from 7.6 billion dollars to 28.5 billions. During the same time, demand deposits of commercial banks (aside from interbank and U. S. Government deposits) increased almost threefold, from 29 billions to 75 billions. If time and governmental deposits are included, total deposits of commercial banks rose almost threefold, from 45 billions to 128 billions. The wartime increases in demand deposits and currency held by individuals and business concerns are shown in Diagram 13 (page 64). They were built upon large purchases of government securities by the banking system.

Each time a bank makes a commercial loan, it credits the deposit account of the borrower, who draws on this new balance at will either by check or in cash. The supply of credit is thus increased by the amount of the loan, less discount. Likewise, a bank buying government obligations, whether bills or bonds, credited a sum equal to it to a Treasury account. The Treasury drew upon this account to pay for munitions and other items, and the recipients usually deposited the money in a bank. Thus, except for some cash withdrawals, most of the money remained in the banking system.

Both bank deposits and currency increased the more the Government borrowed from the banks—or, to put it another way, the more the banks invested in government securities. Part of this increase was warranted by higher employment and payrolls and business levels. But, as Diagram 14 shows, the money supply rose faster than did national income. In the prosperous 1920's, it was about one-third of annual national income; during the uncertain 1930's, it averaged a little less than one-half. World War II raised it to about two-thirds of national income.

DIAGRAM 13

MONEY SUPPLY rose steeply during the war years, both in the hands of individual savers and business concerns.

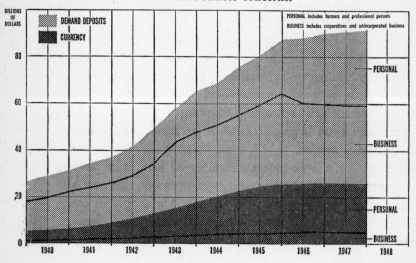

The psychology of the last days of the war and after the war's end was not favorable to the temperate use of money. Prices went up and there was widespread spending. Unsatisfied consumer demands were large; supplies of most goods were inadequate; rationing was terminated; and bottlenecks, shortages and labor troubles affected production. Even before price control was repealed, controls relaxed or were evaded. Meanwhile, retail sales rose to peak levels. After a brief dip, national income passed its wartime peak by the end of 1946 and kept on rising.

What happened is that war inflation followed its usual course. Under the impact of the accumulated huge money supply and other causes, prices bounded upward until they reached the same peak as after World War I—this despite all the differences in conditions.

DIAGRAM 14

MONEY SUPPLY AS PERCENT OF NATIONAL INCOME increased rapidly during the war years, then declined as income continued to rise.

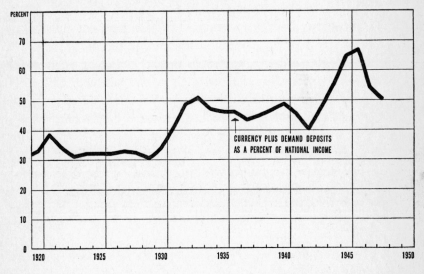

CURRENCY PLUS DEMAND DEPOSITS
AS A PERCENT OF NATIONAL INCOME

One important point to note, however, is that the rise in the money supply has gradually leveled off since the end of the war in 1945. It was held down by government policies which used excess cash built up by the Victory Loan, together with a budget surplus, to pay down government debt held by the banks; a policy of restraint by both Federal Reserve System and Treasury through a modest but continuing increase in money rates; and caution in lending by banks encouraged by a vigorous campaign for this purpose by the American Bankers Association.

At the same time that the money supply was leveling off, the national income was being inflated by rising prices due to accumulated shortages of goods of one sort or another, short crops here and abroad, wage increases, agricultural policies, and the very active efforts of business and government and individuals to rebuild the country. The result is that the ratio of the money supply to the national income shows a sharp dip, as indicated in Diagram 14. This ratio at the end of 1948 is, in fact, nearly back to the levels of the late thirties. Thus the country's economy, measured in dollars, has been catching up with the wartime increase in the money supply.

As this is being written in the beginning of 1949, inflationary pressures are showing signs of weakening. The question is being actively debated whether the spine of the inflation has been definitely broken, or whether inflationary forces will, after a lull, reassert themselves.

In these circumstances the right monetary policy to follow is less clear-cut than it was two years ago, when this section of the report was first drafted. Then the desirable course was to cut down the money supply by vigorous monetary policies, and so dampen the inflationary fires. Today policy must be more flexible. If the inflation peak proves to have been passed, deflationary policies to force reduction in the money supply would be a mistake.

BANKS BECOME INVESTING INSTITUTIONS

We have seen how commercial bank holdings of government obligations expanded by 73 billion dollars during the war, while private loans rose only nine billions. When 1940 began, government securities comprised 40 per cent of all

bank loans and investments; by the end of 1945, the ratio had
nearly doubled to 73 per cent. The banks had become more
investment institutions in government securities than lending
institutions to private enterprise.

Many bankers are concerned about the decline in importance of their lending operations. The great majority of our
14,000 commercial banks were founded to meet the bank
credit needs of commerce, industry, agriculture and responsible individual borrowers. More than a decade ago, many
bankers concluded that the old-fashioned, short-term, self-
liquidating commercial loan was not enough and that they
should expand their lending activities to meet new conditions.
They made loans with maturities as long as ten years. To
meet requirements of borrowers who lacked established credit
standing, they joined in the formation of credit pools. Some
12,000 banks entered the personal loan business to finance
automobile and other consumer goods purchases.

The rise in bank loans since V-J Day shows continued,
active interest in lending functions. By mid-1948, total loans
of insured commercial banks were up 16 billions or almost
70 per cent. Since loans on securities declined almost 4½
billions, the banks have made available to private borrowers
almost 20½ billions. Over half the total went to business and
agriculture; most of the rest was divided between real estate
and consumer loans. These changes are illustrated in Table 5.

During the same time, bank holdings of government securities became 19 billions less—a decline greater than the net
increase in loans and non-governmental securities. Even so,
commercial banks are still more investment than lending institutions. Their mid-1948 government holdings were 57
per cent of their total loans and investments. Despite the increase in private lending operations, government obligations
are likely for many years to compose a larger proportion of

total bank loans and investments than they did before the war. This is one consequence of our huge public debt.

TABLE 5

POSTWAR CHANGES IN LOANS OF INSURED COMMERCIAL BANKS

(Dollar amounts in billions)

	Amount Outstanding		Increase or Decrease (—)	
Loans:	June 30, 1945	June 30, 1948	Amount	Per Cent
Commercial and industrial	$ 7.5	$ 17.8	$10.3	138
Agricultural	1.6	2.0	.3	21
On securities	6.7	2.3	—4.5	—66
Real estate	4.4	10.1	5.7	129
Consumer	2.1	6.4	4.3	204
Other	1.0	1.1	.1	11
Valuation reserves— (deduct)	..	.3	.3	..
Total loans	$ 23.4	$ 39.4	$16.0	69
Investments:				
U. S. Government securities	82.4	63.5	—18.9	—23
Other securities	6.6	8.9	2.4	36
TOTAL LOANS AND INVESTMENTS	$112.4	$111.8	$ —.5	..

CHANGES IN BANK CAPITAL

Capital funds of commercial banks did not keep pace with deposits. Changes from 1929 through 1947 in capital, earnings, deposits, loans and investments of member banks of the Federal Reserve System are shown in Diagram 15. Between 1929 and 1933, banks absorbed such large losses that their capital was reduced by more than a quarter, or 1.75 billions.

DIAGRAM 15

DEPOSITS, LOANS AND INVESTMENTS of member banks more than doubled during the war and are triple those of prosperous 1929

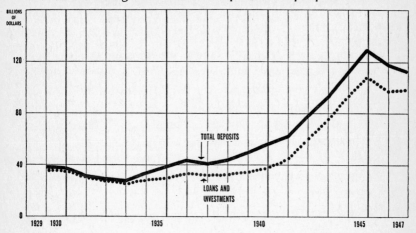

while CAPITAL FUNDS AND NET PROFITS have fallen far behind.

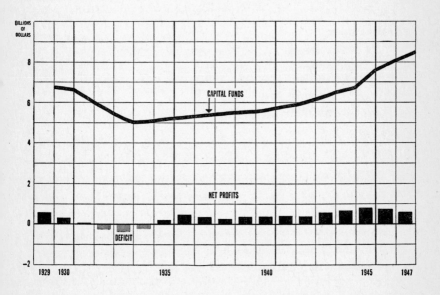

It took a decade, including the profitable years of 1943 and 1944, to bring bank capital back to its 1929 level. At the end of 1947, that capital was one-quarter more than in 1929.

Because money rates continued low, earnings of recent years were not enough to build up bank capital anywhere near as fast as assets and liabilities increased—even though banks distributed only one-third of their earnings as dividends and kept the rest. Some capital increase has come through sale of stock, but the amount is small because bank stocks have been selling below their liquidating values. While bank capital at the end of 1945 was 13 per cent higher than in 1929, deposits were nearly 250 per cent larger. Loans and investments expanded 200 per cent.

TABLE 6

RATIO OF CAPITAL FUNDS TO DEPOSITS AND LOANS AND INVESTMENTS

(Member banks)

| Dec. 31 | Capital Funds as Per Cent of | |
	Deposits	Loans and Investments
1929	17.7	18.7
1941	9.5	13.5
1945	5.9	7.1
1947	6.9	8.7

Thus, as can be seen in Table 6, there was a big decline in the ratio of bank capital to total loans and investments. But what no figures and charts can show is the big improvement since 1929 in the *quality* of bank assets. During and after the war, the banks had several years of excellent earnings and favorable markets for securities and real estate. They made great progress in cutting down doubtful assets left over from depression years of the 1930's. Also, sizeable reductions were made in book values of bank premises. But the most significant of all is that the nearly 90 per cent increase in earning assets since 1929 has been in government securities on which risk is a minimum. So, the decrease in the capital cushion since 1929 is not so serious as the figures might imply. Regarding capital funds as a percentage of "assets at risk," thus excluding cash and government securities, the capital position of commercial banks is now above that of the 1920's, though somewhat lower than it was immediately before the war.

In general, banks were conservative in their purchase of government securities and they greatly increased the percentage of short-term obligations. Almost 45 per cent of the expansion from 1941 through 1945 was in securities maturing in a year or less. At the end of 1945, they were 37 per cent of all government holdings by banks. Short-term retirements starting in 1946 reduced the percentage of issues maturing in one year or less; but at the end of June, 1948, commercial bank assets in short-term Treasury obligations were a considerably larger percentage than in prewar years.

Apparently bank capital is adequate for present needs, but an increase in the future probably is desirable. The volume of bank loans is rising, and holdings of government securities are declining in importance. An adequate margin of stockholder investment is the innermost line of defense for solvency of the banking structure and protection against inevitable losses. But under present conditions, increases in capital are likely to come not from investors but mainly from earnings.

RISE IN BANK EARNINGS

Their expanded holdings of government securities and loans enabled banks to more than cover the large wartime increase in operating expenses and taxes. As a result, their net operating earnings rose during the war and postwar years and by 1947 were more than 80 per cent above what they were before the war. Table 7 reveals profits and losses from 1934 through 1947.

TABLE 7

EARNINGS AND PROFITS DATA FOR IN-SURED COMMERCIAL BANKS, 1934-1947

(Amounts in millions)

	Net Current Operating Earnings (After Income Taxes)	Net Gain or Loss (—) from Profit on Securities and Net Losses and Charge-offs	Net Profit or Loss (—)
1934	$401	$—741	$—340
1935	403	—196	207
1936	441	83	524
1937	467	— 86	381
1938	426	—125	301
1939	446	— 57	389
1940	438	— 37	401
1941	464	— 10	454
1942	489	— 48	441
1943	576	62	638
1944	655	96	751
1945	661	245	906
1946	777	125	902
1947	814	— 32	781

Before the war, bank losses and charge-offs usually were more than profits on security sales, all of which held down net profits. From 1943 through 1946, however, profits on sales of securities plus recoveries of previous losses on loans topped the current losses and charge-offs. This was caused by a rise in the bond market, general increase in real estate and security values and highly satisfactory business conditions.

Under this favorable state of affairs, net profits reached peak levels in 1945 and 1946. Some losses are a normal part of banking, and 1947 losses and charge-offs again exceeded

DIAGRAM 16

EARNINGS OF INSURED COMMERCIAL BANKS
increased in war years largely because of unusual profits from sales of securities at rising prices and also from recoveries on loans previously charged off.

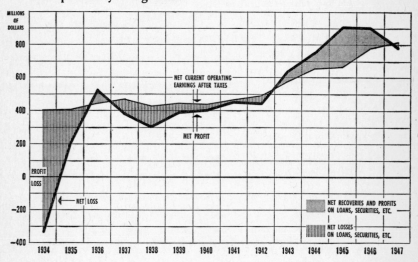

profits on securities and recoveries. Diagram 16 depicts earnings and losses since 1934.

Nevertheless, improved earnings and conservative dividend policies enabled banks to strengthen the capital structures which were so seriously weakened during depression years of the 1930's. And for postwar years, banks have been able to play their essential role in serving business.

BANKS AND POSTWAR GOVERNMENT POLICY

From this review, should be apparent three facts which have major bearing on management of the public debt. It is not enough merely to say that they complicate the problems. To a great extent, they *are* the problems. One is the large amount of federal debt held by the banks. Another is the big proportion of the assets of the banking system which the federal debt represents. Still another is the increased money supply created by expanded bank holdings of federal securities. The influence on national welfare of these three consequences of war finance and policies called for today may be summarized:

1. A basic cause of the postwar inflationary rise in prices and capital values has been the wartime growth in our money supply. The money supply has stopped increasing and leveled off since the end of the war, but high levels of spending by consumers, business, and government have fed on the enlarged money supply and have forced prices up. The country has been catching up with the enlarged money supply.

2. While there are signs that inflationary forces have diminished and some prices are declining, it is not yet clear whether inflation is definitely checked or this is simply a pause in the battle. Some of the inflation pressures continue.

3. Until doubts are clarified certain basic restraints on bank credit should be continued, including: (a) economizing and taxing to create a federal budget surplus which can be used to retire maturing debt held by the banks; (b) selling more securities to the public and using the proceeds to retire debt from the banks; (c) caution in bank lending.

4. The freedom of the Federal Reserve System to use traditional and tested methods of money market management has been limited in the postwar years by the desire of the

Treasury to keep interest rates low and bond prices at par. These objectives need re-examination.

5. Pending a clearer view of the trend, and because of the large powers the Government already has, new grants of more drastic monetary powers for inflation control appear to be unwise.

4

THE DEBT AND INTEREST RATES

INTEREST on the national debt has become an exceedingly large item in the federal budget. Every taxpayer, congressman and administrative official wishes that charge to be as low as possible. In 1941, it was about one billion dollars. In 1948, at about the lowest rates the world has ever seen, it was 5.2 billions. The man who came to dinner remains as a permanent guest.

The problem is bigger than balancing the budget. The influence of interest rates is woven into the Nation's economic fabric. The rates affect the amount of taxes we must pay to carry the public debt. They influence the cost of building and maintaining a home, the amounts businessmen and farmers pay for money they borrow, and what savings banks pay their depositors. Changes in interest rates alter the prices of bonds, stocks, and real estate and play a part in the ups and downs of American business. They determine a man's ability to provide for his old age, for they affect the earnings of life insurance companies and the cost of insurance to millions of policyholders.

It is easy to see how interest on the public debt is an expense to the American people. What we sometimes do not realize is that interest payments are also income for Americans who save. This is true whether we save by depositing in a savings bank, buying government bonds, paying life insurance premiums, contributing to pension plans, or by any other method. Though many questions about interest and the national debt are in the domain of monetary specialists, the size of the national interest bill affects all of us, whether we are aware of it or not.

WHAT ARE INTEREST RATES?

An interest rate is the annual price or rental charge for the use of borrowed money. We speak of interest rates in the plural because there are many different ones, depending mainly upon the risk involved, the loan's purpose and cost of management, and the length of time for which the money is borrowed. These various rates are related to each other, and changes in any one or group are likely to cause readjustment in others.

The levels of rates are determined in a general way by the demand for loans as compared with the supply of funds available. Persons and business concerns borrow for countless reasons; families want to buy homes, automobiles or household equipment, or to pay accumulated bills. Commercial and industrial enterprises borrow to buy buildings and factories, materials or new equipment, or to get working capital. Government borrows in peacetime to finance large public improvements or to provide for the needy. Invariably and stupendously, it borrows in wartime.

The supply of loanable funds is not so obvious as the demand. It is generally believed that the savings of persons and businesses provide all this money. Actually, they are only part of the supply. Another important source is money made available to borrowers by operations of the commercial banking system.

The mechanism of banking operations which raise or lower

the money supply and influence interest rates is one of the most complicated in the whole realm of economics. We need not examine it in detail; but, as explained in Chapter 3, when a commercial bank makes a loan or investment, new bank deposits are at the disposal of the borrower and by that much expand the amount of available money. If banks were perfectly free to expand or contract the supply of bank money, the country would be unduly exposed to dangers of runaway prices, up or down. However, control of this matter is not with the banks, but under the country's central banking system.

FEDERAL RESERVE POLICY AND INTEREST RATES

Almost every country has a central banking organization to insure that the amount of money and its price are determined in the public interest. In the United States, the agency is the Federal Reserve System.

Through its twelve regional banks, the Federal Reserve limits the rate of interest which member banks may pay on time and savings deposits. It raises or lowers the rates at which member banks can borrow at Federal Reserve Banks in order to obtain reserves. By increasing or decreasing its own loans and investments it can raise or lower the amount of cash reserves which member banks hold in Federal Reserve Banks. Within certain limits, it determines what percentage of the demand and time deposits of member banks must be kept in cash reserves with Federal Reserve Banks. At present that proportion for all member banks is about 21 per cent for demand deposits and 7½ per cent for time deposits.

Through its ability to influence the volume of commercial banks' loans and investments and the size of their deposits, the Federal Reserve System exercises wide control over the money supply, which, in turn, influences the movement of interest rates. Therefore, interest rates are not something we must accept like the weather. They can be affected by deliberate central banking policy. But there are limits to the planning and control which can be exercised. The volume of savings is also an important factor, and much still depends on the willingness of people to borrow money; not every horse drinks when led to water.

Subject as our economy is to booms and depressions, Federal Reserve policy has aimed at stabilizing prices, national income and employment at high levels. During boom times, the Federal Reserve has taken steps to tighten up the availability of bank money, mild though they may have been since the war. At such times, its action has encouraged higher interest rates. When prices have fallen and workers have lost their jobs, Federal Reserve policy has favored increased availability of bank money and thereby has been an influence for declining interest rates.

INTEREST RATES IN THE PAST

Until the recent war years, interest rates always fluctuated with the ups and downs of business activity and with changing relationships between demand for loanable funds and their supply. Diagram 17 (page 80) traces the movement of rates from 1858 to 1948 on short-term commercial paper of up to six months. The top and bottom of each column show the highest and lowest monthly rates for the year. The black dot in each column indicates the year's average rate. It will be seen from the diagram that commercial paper rates fluctuated greatly until the early 1930's. They shifted over a considerable range month by month, and their average moved up and down from one year to another, yet between 1875 and 1930 they moved generally within a range of 4 to 6 per cent.

DIAGRAM 17

INTEREST RATES ON COMMERCIAL PAPER had wide fluctuations in most years before the early thirties, then fell to very low and stable levels.

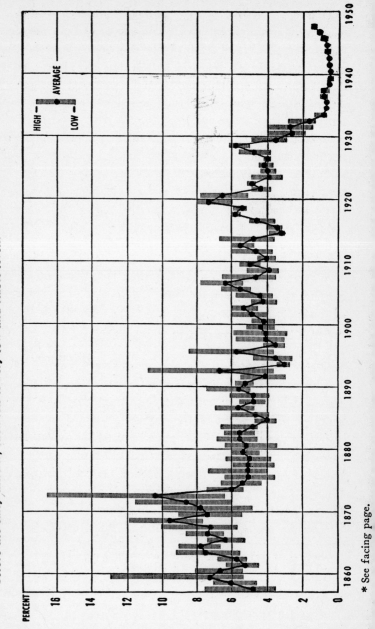

* See facing page.

Diagram 18 (page 82) compares the movement of short-term commercial paper rates and market rates on long-term railroad bonds for the years 1858-1948. Bond rates fluctuated freely from year to year; and, although not shown on the diagram, monthly bond rates varied from month to month as did short-term rates but with more restraint. Because short-term rates have been below long-term ones for nearly two decades, it is commonly assumed that this relationship is a normal one. But as Diagram 18 shows, commercial paper rates were usually above and rarely below those of railroad bonds between 1858 and 1928 and did not remain consistently below until the early 1930's.

DECLINE OF RATES IN THE THIRTIES

Why did short-term interest rates fall so low in the early 1930's and remain there so long? One reason is that for most of the time the American economy—the whole world, in fact —was in a severe depression. With business activity at low ebb, it was natural that demand for loans was less and that both short and long-term interest rates should fall.

This natural tendency was accentuated by the Federal Reserve's deliberate policy of keeping commercial banks freely supplied with reserves and encouraging them to make loans at falling rates. The obvious purpose was to stimulate investment and improve business activity and employment. This policy of easing the borrower's burden also met needs of the United States Treasury: it borrowed heavily in the 1930's to finance relief and public works expenditures.

Another reason for the decline in rates, especially after

---

* Sources of data used in diagram on facing page. Data to 1936 are from F. R. Macaulay's study, *The Movements of Interest Rates, Bond Yields and Stock Prices in the United States since 1856*, National Bureau of Economic Research, 1938. From 1936, from Federal Reserve Board.

DIAGRAM 18

SHORT-TERM COMMERCIAL PAPER RATES were usually above LONG-TERM YIELDS ON RAILROAD BONDS until the sharp decline of the early thirties.

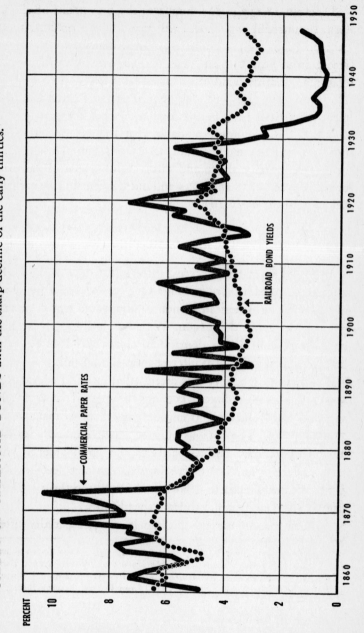

1934, was the large flow of gold into the United States. Between early in that year and late in 1941, the country's gold stock increased from seven billion dollars to 22.7 billions. Largely as a result, the "excess reserves" of the Federal Reserve member banks—those beyond legal requirements—rose steadily from 891 millions in 1934 to 6.8 billions by the end of 1940. While they declined during our national defense program, as 1941 ended and war began they were 3.4 billions, still a high level. This glut of reserves encouraged banks to make short-term investments, chiefly in U. S. securities, at declining rates of interest. Favoring an "easy money" condition, Federal Reserve authorities were content with such an effect during most of the thirties. Short-term rates fell lower and excess reserves continued to increase. To get higher interest rates and keep up their earnings, banks made more long-term investments and thus added to the supply of long-term funds and helped to force down long-term rates.

INTEREST RATES IN WAR FINANCE

For these reasons, the United States entered World War II with interest rates at an unprecedented low level. The question arises as to what rates could and should prevail for financing the war. Memories were fresh of the experience in World War I which was financed on steadily rising rates. Bonds first paid 3½ per cent, then 4 per cent, then 4¼ per cent, and for the Victory Loan of 1919, 4¾ per cent even for a five-year bond. As the rates rose, the bonds which had previously been issued declined in market price. It was necessary to offer bondholders the privilege of exchanging their bonds into the newer issues. This greatly complicated the war financing and increased the cost of borrowing.

As we entered World War II the Treasury took the position, which was supported by financial leaders, that the war should be financed as far as possible at a stable level of interest rates and, since the war promised to be expensive, that the level should be low. According to an agreed pattern, rates were to run from ⅜ of 1 per cent for 90-day Treasury

DIAGRAM 19

YIELDS ON GOVERNMENT SECURITIES

broke away from the wartime pattern in 1945,
pivoted downward to new lows in early 1946.

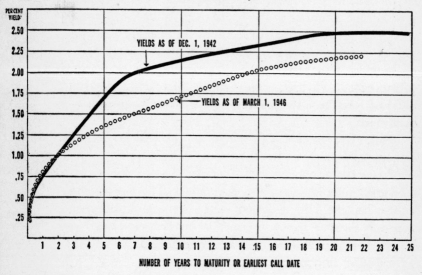

PER CENT YIELD'

YIELDS AS OF DEC. 1, 1942

YIELDS AS OF MARCH 1, 1946

NUMBER OF YEARS TO MATURITY OR EARLIEST CALL DATE

bills, ⅞ of 1 per cent for one-year certificates of indebtedness, and up to 2½ per cent for long-term bonds. These were prevailing market interest rates or security yields, except that shorter-term money rates were a little lower. The black line in Diagram 19 shows the curve of yields on government securities early in the war.

To finance a major war on such a pattern was a gigantic new experiment in monetary control. It required the cooperation of the Treasury, the Federal Reserve System, commercial banks and principal investors. In this financial total war, the country was not alone in results achieved. Somewhat similar ones were reached in Britain, Canada and other countries, but with varying degrees of government control as distinguished from co-operation.

The Federal Reserve System had a two-fold wartime task. One was to see to it that commercial banks always had enough reserves to buy government securities not absorbed by the public. The other was to stabilize market rates on government securities at the established pattern. To further these objectives, Federal Reserve Banks took the steps described in the preceding chapter. They made bank holdings of Treasury bills practically the equivalent of cash reserves to the banker and they gave him a preferentially low rate of ½ of 1 per cent for borrowing on short-term government securities.

Besides co-operation with the banks, the Federal Reserve System undertook, as we have seen, to support by market purchases the prices of issued securities. Thus, prices as well as market interest rates were maintained. This pegging operation had the help of dealers in government securities who kept the Reserve Banks informed of market conditions and worked with them and the Treasury in maintaining the agreed-upon rate pattern.

On the whole, and for most of the war, the program went forward as planned. The war was financed at stable rates. Investors had confidence in the market, every Treasury issue was fully subscribed, and each bond drive did better than the one before. The Treasury sold to non-bank investors about 60 per cent of all securities issued, and expansion of bank credit was kept within bounds.

Whether or not the results were as good as might have been under another pattern of rates, no one can say. If bonds at a somewhat higher rate had been sold, possibly still more might have been taken and kept by non-bank investors and less might have been placed in commercial banks. As for the small investor, the Treasury offered savings bonds at a considerably more attractive rate than what prevailed in the market. Series E bonds carried a rate averaging 2.9 per cent if held for ten years.

PATTERN MAINTAINED UNTIL 1945

The program was far from perfect. As months went on, investors and particularly the banks grew almost too confident in the power of the Federal Reserve and the Treasury to maintain stable rates and prices for government securities. This led to increased speculation. By 1945, people found that they could buy longer-term securities when they were issued and sell them later at a profit. Investors or speculators regarded these bonds as just as safe as short-term ones because, with government-maintained prices, there was almost no risk of loss. As a result, too much of what should have been short-term money was put into longer-term bonds. It became too much of a good thing.

Under such conditions, market interest rates on government securities broke in 1945, as shown in Diagram 20. Prices rose so that the return at market price on medium-term 2 per cent bonds fell to $1\frac{1}{4}$ per cent in the spring of 1946. Other maturities had similar but not such wide declines in yield. Their downward pivot, as shown in Diagram 19's broken line, was encouraged by market interpretations of Treasury statements as presaging still lower rates.

By the spring of 1946, the Federal Reserve expressed concern. Chairman Marriner S. Eccles said: ". . . it is important to point out that so long as the public debt continues to be monetized through the purchase of government securities by the banking system, the supply of money will continue to increase, thus tending further to reduce the interest rate on savings and investment funds. The resultant pressure of an increasing money supply and of lower interest

DIAGRAM 20

GOVERNMENT SECURITY YIELDS held firmly through. 1944, then declined on medium and longer term and finally rose, with short-term rates leading.

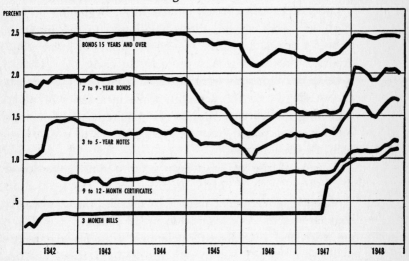

rates is bound to have a further inflationary effect upon all capital assets and to increase the difficulty of holding down the cost of living." [5]

A number of steps were taken to prevent further decline in rates and to halt expansion of bank credit caused by bank purchases of government bonds. The Federal Reserve Banks raised from ½ of 1 per cent to a full 1 per cent the rate at which banks could borrow on short-term government securi-

[5] *Federal Reserve Bulletin*, February, 1946, p. 121.

ties. About the same time, the Treasury drew on its large cash balance, mostly held in the member banks, to pay off its maturing securities. From the February, 1946, peak, to the end of that year, the debt was reduced by about 20 billions. A large part of these securities were in Federal Reserve Banks. The money was thus drawn from member banks and paid in to the Reserve Banks, so that bank reserves were put under pressure. Debt retirement continued but out of tax receipts in 1947 and 1948.

Other steps also affected interest rates. Beginning in July, 1947, the Treasury bill rate was allowed to rise by stages to over 1 per cent, and the rate on certificates of indebtedness gradually increased to 1¼ per cent. In early 1948 Federal Reserve discount rates were increased from 1 to 1¼ per cent, and in August to 1½ per cent, while in a series of moves beginning in February the reserve requirements of member banks were increased from an average of 18 to over 21 per cent of demand deposits.

A general rise of short-term interest rates accompanied these steps, with a notable broadening in the market for short-term government securities outside the commercial banking system. As demand for capital funds increased during 1947 and 1948 long-term interest rates likewise tended to become firmer; but though the Federal Reserve Banks forced a sharp readjustment by reducing their support prices for government securities in December, 1947, they continued to hold the long-term government bond market at 2½ per cent.

Control over interest rates and a stable rate pattern were essential in the general wartime governmental control over our national economy. But the question now arises whether such control is appropriate for our peacetime economy. What interest policy would best promote the national welfare in the future? Should government continue to control interest rates and encourage lower rates than those now prevailing? Or is some other policy better and feasible?

THE CASE FOR LOWER RATES

For several years, a policy of lower interest rates was strongly advocated in government and academic circles, both here and abroad. This sentiment, however, waned considerably as the inflationary spiral wound higher and higher. But since the policy had many adherents, any downturn in business is likely to see it urged again.

The argument for a government policy of lower interest rates has two chief points. One is that the obvious way to reduce the huge interest charge on our national debt is to drive rates still lower. For example, at an average rate of 2 per cent, the annual interest charge on a public debt of 250 billion dollars would be five billions. But at an average rate of 1½ per cent, interest on the same debt would be 3.75 billions.

A second claim is that falling rates would stimulate business activity and high employment. This assumes that the interest rate is a major consideration in decisions to borrow. The lower the rates, it is reasoned, the greater the encouragement for businessmen to undertake new ventures and expand old ones, to borrow for new factory buildings and equipment and fresh stocks of goods—all of which would provide more jobs.

DISADVANTAGES OF LOWER RATES

One argument against lower interest rates is that it adds to inflationary pressure. The chief means by which government induces lower rates is to keep commercial banks so well supplied with reserves that they buy longer-term government securities at rising prices and falling market interest rates. Such a policy would lodge more federal debt in the banks and increase still further bank deposits which comprise the general public's major money supply. This is particularly dangerous in an inflationary period when government policy should be reduction of the money supply. It should then sell more long-term bonds to investors and use the proceeds to retire part of the public debt held by banks. But to sell bonds to investors, an attractive rate is necessary.

The case for lower rates fails to cover the whole situation. It views interest charges as a *cost* to society and overlooks the fact that federal interest payments also make up part of the *income* of society. Although further reductions in interest rates may save people as taxpayers, they penalize people as recipients of interest income.

For example, life insurance costs depend heavily upon the level of interest rates. Premium payments go into reserves, and the compounding of interest on those reserves creates a large part of payments to beneficiaries. Lewis W. Douglas, present Ambassador to Great Britain, testified in 1945 while president of the Mutual Life Insurance Company of New York before the Senate Banking and Currency Committee, that between 1930 and 1944 the gross rate of interest earned by a large group of insurance companies fell from 5.31 to 3.57 per cent.[6] This drop meant, he pointed out, that to provide the same dollar value of life insurance protection, premium payments were one-sixth higher in 1944 than they were in 1930. Moreover, Mr. Douglas warned that the one-sixth increase in life insurance costs would become one-third should interest rates drop another percentage point. The

[6] *Housing, Interest Rates, and the Cost of Life Insurance,* testimony of Lewis W. Douglas before the Senate Banking and Currency Committee, December 17, 1945. (Printed by the Life Insurance Investment Research Committee.)

gross rate earned by life insurance companies did fall to 2.87 per cent in 1947, and the effect of this impact will be discussed in a later chapter.

OTHER ADVERSE EFFECTS

Lower interest rates penalize the American people in more ways than one. They reduce the investment earnings of savings banks and thus cut the interest paid to millions of savings depositors. In the past fifteen or twenty years, interest paid to savings depositors has dropped from 3½ and 4 per cent to 1½ and 2 per cent. Incomes of beneficiaries of trust funds have likewise been affected.

Falling interest rates increase the cost of pension plans which business concerns have set up for millions of employees. They also affect the retirement funds of teachers, policemen, other municipal employees and clergymen. Thirty annual payments of $500, or $15,000 in all, create at 4½ per cent interest a pension reserve of $31,876. To create a pension reserve of the same size at a 2¾ per cent rate would require annual contributions of $679, or 36 per cent more. Moreover, in 1930, when a pension reserve of $31,876 could be built from annual payments of $500, a man reaching 65 could expect from it monthly payments of $273. In 1947, his pension would have been about $194 a month.

Those who save to buy annuities for their old age cannot get the incomes they might have had in the past. Between 1933 and 1946, annuity costs rose 50 to 70 per cent. Although lengthened life expectancies have had some effect, the greater part of increased annuity costs is due to reduced interest rates.

Savings bank deposits, annuities, pensions, endowment policies—all these forms of savings are of great social value.

All are clipped by one or both blades of the scissors of declining interest rates. Not only are their incomes less, but the dollars from these funds do not buy as good a living as formerly.

The incomes of educational institutions, research foundations and religious and charitable bodies are largely from investments. Consider the effect of falling interest rates on one of these great agencies of public service. The Carnegie Corporation of New York was founded for education, scientific research and social welfare purposes. Largely because of lower returns from interest, its endowment income available for use in this country declined from $6,637,072 in 1932 to $3,989,590 in 1945—a drop of 40 per cent. "Under such circumstances," the corporation's president, Devereaux C. Josephs, reported in 1944 "[the trustees] are convinced of their obligation to discontinue many continuing or recurrent grants as well as to limit the number and extent of new ones."

After 1945 the corporation's income was increased by more than $1,200,000, partly because of the sale of part of its government bonds, the purchase of higher-yielding securities and the rise in dividends. But this increase did not enable Carnegie Corporation to regain its lost income level, and the experience is typical of the severe curtailment of funds available for expenditure by foundations.

Severe though that curtailment is already, savings banks, life insurance companies and other institutions have not felt fully the effect of today's low interest rates. Nor will they do so until the bonds, preferred stocks and mortgages in their portfolios mature or are called and refunded. Nevertheless, we have seen how lower interest rates reduce the tax load, but directly and indirectly diminish returns on savings and reduce the incomes of essential institutions. It is a fair question whether lower rates are more a burden to society than a relief.

DO LOWER RATES AID INVESTMENT?

In the past many economists believed that the cost of borrowed money was an important factor in decisions of businessmen to expand their operations. Today, however, economists are swinging to the view that business enterprise is not greatly stimulated by falling interest rates, especially by further reduction in rates already low. This position is outlined in the following statement by Professor John Maurice Clark in the Twentieth Century Fund's *Financing American Prosperity* (pp. 110-111):

> "A low interest rate can have a material stimulus to investment in some important areas where maintenance and depreciation are low, risks are moderate, and interest is really a substantial part of the cost incurred on account of an investment of capital. This is pre-eminently true of hydro-electric installations, and it is broadly true of housing. But in the general field of industry and trade, low interest rates cannot accomplish as much as many economic theorists give them credit for. Interest alone is a minor part of the total cost or sacrifice involved in capital outlay, especially in a dynamic industry where equipment gets obsolete long before it is worn out and allowance for obsolescence alone dwarfs the element of interest."

The contention that low interest rates are a strong stimulus to housing construction is questioned in a careful study by Professor C. D. Long, *Building Cycles and the Theory of Investment,* in which he states (p. 29):

". . . we must come to the conclusion that under the most extreme circumstances interest can only exercise a minor role in the inducement to invest in residential buildings. What is true of the more durable residential building must be even more true of the less durable non-residential building, except notably for public building and building in certain protected industries."

A recent study of *Housing Costs* of the National Housing Administration supports Professor Long's conclusion. Changes in the cost of building, the availability of funds and labor, and taxes are more decisive factors in building than interest rates.

Experience indicates that when profit expectations are good, business enterprisers are willing to pay high rates for borrowed funds, but when the expectations are bad, low interest does very little to stimulate business borrowing and spending. It is certain that changes in the wages and taxes, for example, are much more influential factors than interest in decisions of businessmen to borrow and spend money. Changes in interest rates, especially rising rates at the top of a boom, have an influence in these decisions, but their importance on the whole has been exaggerated. Indeed, the ease or difficulty of access to borrowed money is a more important factor than the height of interest rates.

IS SOME OTHER POLICY BETTER?

It seems clear that still lower interest rates would be unwise both now and in the future. If applied now, there is the danger that they would restimulate inflationary pressures. As a long-range policy, further reduction of interest rates would neither promote business expansion and housing construction nor afford a real saving to the American people.

Consideration of any future policy, however, must rest on the realistic assumption that the Government will continue to have a regulating effect on interest rates.

There are important reasons for that regulation. Ever since a centralized banking authority was established in 1914, it has been recognized that the Federal Reserve System's control over the volume of bank deposits and interest rates can be an influence for high-level, stable business activity. Today, when a huge national debt occupies so central a place in our national economy, need for some government influence over interest rates is even greater.

But that control must be guided by a policy which includes the general welfare as much as the well-being of the Treasury. We suggest that the control should not be so rigid as it was during the war. It should be elastic enough to allow adjustment of rates to quickly changing conditions in our peacetime economy, and according to three guiding principles.

AN ELASTIC POLICY

1. Interest rates should be flexible enough to enable credit control to have a part in curbing inflation or resisting deflation. When inflationary forces are strong, the public welfare may be served best by taking up slack in the money market. Tighter credit means inevitably higher interest rates. But when prices fall and unemployment spreads, an easier credit policy and lower rates at least can help to relieve tension.

How much change an effective credit policy calls for in the way of availability of bank credit and of interest rates cannot be determined exactly in advance. Of course, credit policy is only one of many factors affecting economic change. Tightened credit does more to check expansion than easy credit aids recovery, and there is always the possibility of inflationary conditions arising which require sizable changes in credit policy and rates. Again and again, however, experience has shown that when proper steps are taken in time, moderate changes in the availability of credit and moderate rate changes are helpful in governing business and price fluctuations.

A level and a pattern of interest rates cannot be picked arbitrarily out of the air and as arbitrarily adhered to. They must fit conditions. The guide is not whether they conform to any theory of high or low rates, but whether in actual practice they harmonize with the main monetary and credit objectives. Above all, monetary authorities must not become so obsessed with rate reduction or one pattern of rates as to bring on inflation or deflation. An outstanding example of this danger is the Federal Reserve System's very long continued purchase of Treasury bills, certificates and bonds at pegged rates. It is hard to escape the conviction that this policy added to inflationary pressures.

2. Government control over interest rates should be in full awareness that interest is *both* a cost to society and a part of its income. Almost all discussions of interest put too much emphasis on the tax cost of charges on our national debt; the income aspect is usually neglected.

On the income side of interest rates, we face the question of a *fair return to savers*. Americans have always provided for "rainy days" through their own savings. If this healthy custom is to continue and government does not take over completely the provision against all hazards of life—or attempt to do so—then it is essential that savers receive a fair reward. This is a "human right." It merits as much consideration as is given the borrower of money.

A closely allied danger is that an arbitrary policy of driving interest rates lower will jeopardize the effectiveness of such American institutions as life insurance companies, savings banks, pension funds, research foundations and religious and charitable groups. All of these organizations perform valuable services in our society. No interest-rate policy should be decided upon without full consideration of their needs and through them the needs of American savers.

3. Interest rates should have some freedom of movement. Without it, they cannot perform their economic function of maintaining a balance between the supply of savings and demand for investment funds at a high and increasing level of national income. A popular theory has been that the American people "oversave"—that they choke off prosperity by withholding too much money from consumer purchases. The great demand for investment funds which now exists and is likely to continue for many years, compels readjustment of attitude towards savings. Our nation has enjoyed a rising standard of living largely because abundant savings built up a great industrial system and enabled us to produce more and more goods and services. If living standards are to continue to improve, we must have adequate savings; and this is partly a question of the right level of interest rates. No one knows what the right rates are going to be, but the best chance of getting them will be when rates are flexible enough to reflect the market forces of demand for savings and their supply.

If these goals are kept firmly in mind, government interest-rate policy can make important contribution to the general welfare. But if the Government uses its control over rates simply to hold down the debt service charge and ignores other aspects of interest rates, it may destroy much that is good in our enterprise economy. It would sacrifice an important part of America's incentive to save to the expediency of the budget; and although results might be long delayed, they would be extremely serious when they caught up with us.

5

THE DEBT AND OUR SAVINGS

THE economic history of the United States is a story of phenomenal advance in living standards of the people. From the era of tallow candles and horse-drawn carriages to the day of fluorescent tubes and streamlined motor cars, America has moved toward higher and higher planes of living. More and more, and better and better goods and services have poured into our markets in an ever-expanding stream. The average man has fewer hours of toil, vastly improved facilities of life, and multiple opportunities for education, culture, health and recreation.

Dry figures cannot do justice to this achievement of the American economy. However, a rough indication of our rapid progress in living standards is the fact that "real" per capita income—income, that is, measured by dollars of constant purchasing power—in this country rose from $216 in 1799 to about $900 in 1947. Even these figures tell us nothing about the immensely improved quality of goods and services—of the change, for example, from the old-fashioned ice box to the modern mechanical refrigerator.

Not all of our economic progress has been in more and better products and service. Americans have also chosen increased leisure. The average work week in manufacturing industries declined from sixty-four hours in 1849 to about forty in 1948. Correspondingly the facilities for culture and recreation expanded. In 1870, only 57 per cent of those between five and seventeen years of age attended public schools. In 1942, attendance was 84.2 per cent. The average expenditure per pupil rose during that time from $15.55 to $110.03. Similarly, the number completing a four-year high school course rose from a mere 16,000 in 1870 to 1,242,375 in 1942, and those graduating from college increased from 9,371 to 185,346 in the same period.

What has this record to do with savings and the national debt? The answer is that this progress is largely due to the frugality of the American people and the productive use of their savings. Our industrial system was blessed with abundant natural resources, freedom of opportunity, men richly endowed with effective "know-how," and a huge domestic market free of tariff barriers, all of which played important parts in our economic progress. However, the fundamental explanation for the rapid improvement in living standards lies in the fact that the American people and business concerns have saved and invested wisely large amounts of their incomes. Savings put to work as capital are the secret of our steady march to higher planes of living.

SAVINGS AND NATIONAL DEBT

There are a number of links between savings and the national debt. First, debt operations have a direct effect on the volume of savings. When the Government expands its debt, as during war, the public's money supply increases by the amount of federal securities sold to the commercial banking system. An expanded money supply, in turn, tends to increase the number of dollars saved, even though it may likewise contribute to rising prices, and thus to a decline in the value of the dollars saved. On the other hand, when the Government operates at a budgetary surplus by collecting more in taxes than it spends, and bank-held debt is being paid off, the money supply of the Nation tends to be reduced. With a falling money supply the number of dollars saved tends to decrease.

Secondly, through the effect of the debt on prices, the Government changes the purchasing power of accumulated savings. Changes in prices also influence both the ability and the inducement to save.

Finally, by means of debt management and monetary policy the Government affects interest rates and thus has some further influence on the inducement to save.

SAVINGS AND ECONOMIC PROGRESS

The essence of personal saving is that individuals refrain from spending their entire current income, but for countless reasons choose instead to lay aside a certain part for future needs.

Normally, income held back from consumption does not result merely in the piling up of idle or hoarded funds. The accumulations of those who save are always accompanied by more or less "dissaving" by others who voluntarily or from necessity draw on past savings or borrow to finance consumption expenditures. Also, savings are put to a productive use, or *invested*. The farmer uses his savings to build a new barn or perhaps to purchase a tractor; the industrial worker may employ his savings to build a house. These two cases illustrate direct investment of savings by individuals. Actually, the saving process takes a myriad of forms.

A great part of personal savings is channeled through mutual savings banks, savings departments of commercial banks, life insurance companies, and savings and loan associations. These institutions manage the savings of individuals and put them to work by lending funds to other individuals, industrial firms, public utility companies, railroads, home builders, and government. For example, people deposit in mutual savings banks; the banks, in turn, invest these savings in real estate mortgages and various kinds of industrial and government bonds. Out of their investment earnings the banks are able to pay interest to the original savings depositor.

Not all saving is done by individuals. It is common practice today for American business concerns to put aside part of their earnings to carry necessary stocks of goods, to build new plants and install new and improved machinery. The fact to note is that no matter how they accumulate in the United States, the savings usually go into productive use through investment. They make possible the production of durable "producer goods" that last for years—industrial plants, machinery, public utility plants, railroads. They are the source of the tools with which a better civilization is built.

SAVINGS AND PRODUCTION

The National Industrial Conference Board estimated that the savings invested per wage-earner for the buildings and tools of manufacturing industry (computed to allow for price changes) increased from about $1,020 in 1849 to approximately $5,860 in 1942—nearly a sixfold increase. These figures are in terms of the value of the dollar in 1926. As a result of this expanded investment, each wage-earner in 1939 (last year for which figures were available) had an average of 6.4 horsepower to work with, as compared with only 1.3 in 1849. It is not surprising, therefore, that the "value added by manufacture" per wage-earner, in terms of 1926 prices, rose from about $850 in 1849 to about $5,460 in 1944. Here is a measure of the enormous increase in the joint product of labor, managerial skill, and capital equipment.

Department of Labor figures for a shorter period indicate that the output per man-hour in all manufacturing industries increased 263 per cent from 1909 to 1939. This steadily improving productivity with better tools is the basic reason why "real" hourly earnings (in terms of 1923-1925 purchasing power) of manufacturing workers increased from an average of about 25 cents in 1849 to 94.5 cents in 1947, and "real" weekly earnings rose from about $16.00 to $38.10 during the same period.

In short, without savings, our amazing industrial system never would have developed. Without savings, Americans would not be the best housed people in the world, a condition which is true despite our present shortages. Savings made possible the more rapid exploitation of inventions which have paved the way to higher living plateaus. Finally, savings have contributed to the development of a mass distribution system by which the fruits of our increased productivity are quickly and conveniently made available to consumers everywhere in the country.

SAVINGS STILL URGENTLY NEEDED

It may be argued whether saving has not outlived its usefulness for the United States. Have we not moved to so high a plane of living that saving is no longer essential? Do we not already produce so many goods and services that our people cannot consume all of them? Would it not be better if Americans stopped saving and consumed the full fruit of their production?

On the contrary, there is evidence that savings are more urgently needed today than ever before. Who can say that the American plane of living has reached the point where we either cannot or need not progress further? Even today, with the highest national income in history, per capita income is only about $1,500, a sum which reflects the sharp increase of prices in recent years. Despite our great progress, Americans of all sorts and conditions are pressing for greater real wages and higher living standards.

Our wants and desires for foodstuffs could be fulfilled eventually, for there is a limit to the size of our stomachs. But when we consider other types of consumer goods such as automobiles, electric washing machines, radios, television sets, and the whole myriad of goods constructed by our inventive genius, whenever we think of the multiplicity of services which contribute to leisure and enjoyment in modern living, we realize that the wants and desires of Americans are insatiable. There is still an enormous unsatisfied demand for these goods, and a great new desire will spring up for the new products we shall develop in coming years. New housing alone will require a huge amount of saving. Moreover, the craving for even more leisure, recreation, education and better health will call for more saving. Clearly there is pressing need in this country for further savings.

American savings are required not only in this country. They are equally essential for reconstruction and industrial development abroad. If we are to lay the basis for a lasting world peace, some of our savings should, when conditions are ripe, flow into foreign countries to assist in the restoration and development of their economies. Through the use of our savings, and thus by means of higher productivity, foreign countries will move to better standards of living. This will mean a greater exchange of products with us. It will contribute to a further improvement in our living standards. It will be a step towards a peaceful world.

The only way for *any* country on the globe to enjoy better living standards is through savings and investment. This is just as true of communist Russia or socialist Britain as it is of capitalist America. The very essence of Russia's prewar five-year plans was the increase of productive capacity at the expense of consumer goods. Saving was forced on the Russian people by the central industrial planners, but it was saving nonetheless. Likewise in Britain today, the people are being frugal in the interests of restoring and developing their industrial system. Thus, saving is the universal way to progress in living standards.

THE "OVERSAVING" THESIS

During the thirties an influential school of economic thought in this country and abroad held that the basic cause of the depression was "oversaving." Even today many economists fear that "oversaving" will eventually lead us into another deep, prolonged depression. Although there are many variations to the "oversaving" thesis, two versions of the argument are most frequently encountered.

Some economists contend that as personal incomes rise during an upward swing of the business cycle, people save a larger percentage of their incomes and reduce proportionately their expenditures. At the same time, this lag in the purchase of goods and services lessens the demand for investment funds to finance industrial growth. So, it is argued, with the people as a whole trying to save at a rate exceeding the demand for investment funds, the stream of income flowing through the economy shrinks, and depression ensues.

This theory rests on two assumptions. One is that individual saving and spending habits always follow a "set" pattern. Actually, who knows whether or not they will? Consumer spending habits may be changed by huge accumulations of liquid assets and the availability of consumer credit. If, for example, people have large back-logs of savings they may, in defiance of the "oversaving" theory, spend their current incomes more freely, borrow on installment, and thus create an actual excess of spending and inflation. A second assumption is that the demand for investment funds depends entirely on the rate of consumer expenditures. The fact is that many other influences enter into the demand for capital funds, notably the rate at which important new inventions are being developed.

Another variation of the "oversaving" theory—more often heard during the depressed thirties than today—is the "mature economy" doctrine. The American economy, it was contended, has developed so far that without the impetus of large scale public expenditures, there are no longer adequate outlets for constantly accumulating savings. In support of this thesis proponents cited the "vanishing" frontier and a slack in population growth. Much was said also of the "absence" of important new technological changes or inventions on the horizon which promised to use large amounts of savings, and the "lack" of new industries like the railroads or automobiles awaiting development. Thus the conclusion was drawn that the American economy faces "secular stagnation" or long-lasting unemployment and depression. American savings, it was said, would lie idle for lack of private investment opportunities, and force the Government to step in with "compensatory" spending to keep the economy moving ahead.

The pitfalls in the "compensatory" budget were marked in Chapter 2, and this is not the place for lengthy criticism of the stagnation thesis. Dr. George Terborgh has provided such a discussion in his excellent study *The Bogey of Economic Maturity*. Sufficient to note that most economists today regard the thesis of "secular stagnation" as still in the realm of unproved theory. Economic developments of the next few decades might give us more positive evidence one way or the other. But the theory is so much a product of the great depression that the history of economic thought may record the "oversaving" and "mature economy" arguments of the thirties as one more expression of the pessimistic philosophy which originated with T. R. Malthus in the early nineteenth century and which crops up again and again in every depression period.

Today at least, the theory runs quite contrary to evidence. There is every indication that a large volume of private investment will still be required for several years to fill the backlog of consumer and producer demand built up during the war, to satisfy housing needs, and to exploit the accumulation of new inventions.

Beyond that time, the shattering wartime scientific discoveries offer good ground for confidence that private investment outlets will readily absorb our savings. We do not need an expanding frontier and a rapidly growing population to provide investment opportunities. Further intensive development of our country and higher living standards can require a huge amount of capital without reliance upon a heavy public spending program. In the future, as in the past, there may be temporary economic setbacks. But even these might be kept at a minimum if government policies are such as to foster an economic environment which encourages pioneering Americans to go ahead with new business ventures.

In the August 10, 1947, New York *Times* Magazine, Professor Sumner Slichter of Harvard University termed the belief that we are becoming dangerously thrifty as one of the eight errors in our current economic thinking. Pointing to the need for savings, he wrote:

> "Today the United States is grievously short of plant and equipment. . . . For many years the private plant and equipment of the country have been from one and one-half to two times as large as the annual output of industry. At the present time plant and equipment are just about the size of the annual output of industry. The pre-war ratio between plant and equipment on the

one hand and the output of industry on the other may never be restored, but it is safe to estimate that the country is short at least $40 billion of capital and probably much more. The country needs to encourage the formation of capital, and savings are needed in order to make this possible."

This statement prompts the question: What are the facts about saving?

SOME FACTS ABOUT SAVINGS

Information about American savings, though incomplete, shows how deeply saving for the future is ingrained in our way of life. We are a thrifty people. Nearly everyone in this country is a saver in one form or another—saving is by no means reserved for the rich man.

Diagram 21 (page 108) charts perhaps the most reliable estimates of the gross national income, gross national savings including those of corporations as well as individuals, and gross savings as a percentage of gross national income. The data and sources are given in Table 11 in the Appendix. The figures indicate a strong tendency for savings to fluctuate with national income. They also demonstrate the strong tendency for Americans to save. The very high figures of the war years reflect the piling up of the inflated money supply in savings at a time many wartime consumer goods were restricted and scarce. Conversely, the postwar decline is partly the effect of spending for goods then becoming available.

Among various surveys of savings in different income groups is one made in 1946 for the Board of Governors of the Federal Reserve System and the Department of Agriculture. Those with incomes of $5,000 and over in 1941 were credited with about 68 per cent of all personal savings. In

DIAGRAM 21

GROSS NATIONAL SAVINGS (in 1929 dollar values), generally moving with national income, have declined sharply from the wartime peak.

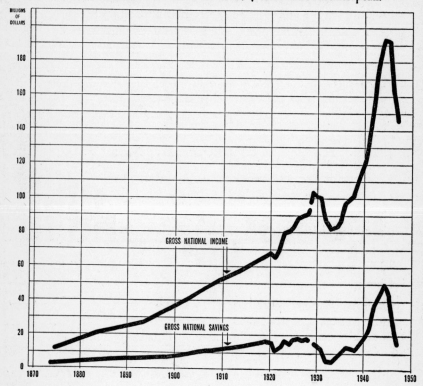

Figures from 1869 to 1918 are averages per year by decades.

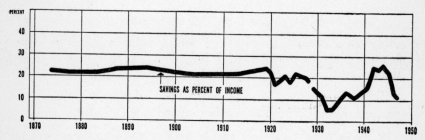

For numerical data, see Table 11, Appendix.

1945, they laid aside 40 per cent of the total. In 1947, the proportion rose to over 80 per cent. Of course, by 1947 the number of people receiving $5,000 a year and over was much greater than in earlier years, but it is clear enough that the

DIAGRAM 22

CORPORATE SAVINGS which have been large in recent years are used to finance expansion and strengthen enterprise.

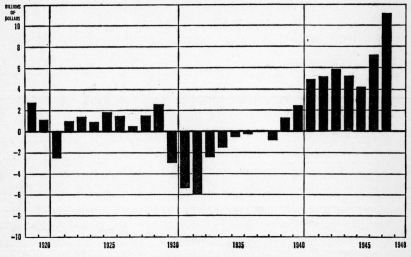

Old series of Department of Commerce used from 1919 to 1928; new series used from 1929 to 1947. On old basis, corporate savings in 1929 were 1.3 billion dollars.

bulk of savings is usually by families with larger incomes.

At the other end of the scale, it was noted in 1945 that families in the income brackets under $1,000 saved nothing as a group. There is even reason to believe that taken together these families actually had deficits in their personal budgets, particularly if excess expenditures financed by consumer credit are taken into account. A large number of the families in this group were living on their accumulated resources, and since obviously no one can live indefinitely above his means, others were temporarily reduced to this low income status. One-third of the heads of households in this group were retired, unemployed, or housewives. They were living on past savings, or public assistance, or the proceeds of life insurance policies, or on servicemen's allotments. Still others were recipients of irregular incomes, such as authors and professional men. Another fact surveys brought out is that, although many low income families spend on the average more than their income, the typical family actually sets aside small savings in the form of war bonds and premiums.

Another significant fact is that a good portion of the country's savings is made by corporations. They are laying by for expansion, improved plant and equipment, new inventories, and to strengthen the company's position against bad times. Diagram 22 (page 109) shows Department of Commerce figures for corporate savings between 1919 and 1947. Its data and sources are given in Table 12 in the Appendix. The positive savings in the chart represent net income retained by corporations after tax and dividend payments. The negative amounts, concentrated in the depressed thirties, indicate payments made by corporations out of previously accumulated assets instead of out of income.

THE FLOW OF SAVINGS THROUGH INSTITUTIONS

Each year Americans channeled more and more savings into such financial institutions as life insurance companies, mutual savings banks, insured commercial banks, and savings and loan associations. Diagram 23 shows how these savings have piled up since 1920.

Life insurance growth has been rapid. The face value of all legal reserve life insurance in force has increased from 8.6 billion dollars at the end of 1900 to about 201 bil-

lions on residents of the continental United States at the
close of 1948. During the same time assets of the companies
have grown from 1.7 billions to about 55 billions.

DIAGRAM 23

VOLUME OF INDIVIDUAL LONG-TERM SAVINGS
in selected types of investment has increased
steadily and in late years rapidly.

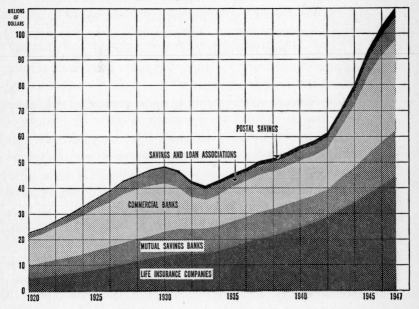

For numerical data, see Table 12, Appendix.

Moreover, life insurance is providing a service not only to
people in the upper income brackets, but also to the general
mass of low and middle-income families of the country. In
1945, about 96 per cent of the claims paid under ordinary
life policies were for $10,000 or less, and these claims were
71 per cent of the claims paid under ordinary life. If group
and industrial policies were added, the ownership of life in-

surance by low and middle-income groups would be an even greater proportion.

Deposits in mutual savings banks increased sharply from 4.8 billion dollars on December 31, 1920, to 10.6 billions at the end of 1940 and 17.8 billions at the close of 1947. These banks, which operate in only seventeen states, have almost 18 million accounts, owned by men and women in all walks of life. The average account at the end of 1946 was $946. But deposits in mutual savings banks are only part of the total savings deposits in this country. If we add the time deposits of commercial banks, which are largely thrift accounts, we find that on June 30, 1945, there were almost 50,000,000 savings accounts.

Consider one more institution which manages savings—the trust company. An American Bankers Association study in 1947 disclosed that 868 reporting trust companies out of a total of 2,800 were administering 144,081 trusts for beneficiaries—mostly women and children. The typical trust serves persons of comparatively moderate means. Over 73 per cent of the 144,081 trusts reported provided incomes of less than $3,000 a year. More than half were incomes under $1,200 a year. Only 2.8 per cent of the trusts yielded annual incomes above $25,000.

These facts show how savings institutions serve as funnels into which a large part of the savings of Americans is poured. The bulk of these institutions are "mutual" or nonprofit-making in nature, and others operate on narrow profit margins. Hence, in the long run, almost the full investment return goes to the original savers or to their beneficiaries.

It has already been pointed out that savings normally find their way into productive uses and thereby build up our industrial capacity and improve our living standards. Table 8 gives an idea of the many uses to which savings accumulated in institutions have been directed in recent years. A large part of the funds have gone into United States Government bonds, and substantial amounts have found their way into the stocks and bonds of industrial corporations, public utilities, and railroads, and into real estate mortgages. The next question is what effect government policies in recent years have had upon those savings.

TABLE 8

PERCENTAGE OF ACCUMULATED SAVINGS DIRECTED BY SELECTED INSTITUTIONS INTO VARIOUS INVESTMENT OUTLETS IN 1947

Investment Outlet	Mutual Savings Banks	Saving and Loan Associations	Life Insurance Companies
Bonds *	68.73	14.98	73.1
Preferred stock of corporations ⎱	0.74	0.97	1.9
Common stock of corporations ⎰			0.5
Real estate mortgages	25.08	77.98	15.5
Real estate	0.07	0.07 ⎱	1.6
Investment in institutional property	0.47	0.75 ⎰	
Personal loans and notes	. . .	. . .	3.6
Other	0.41	0.43	2.0
Uninvested cash	4.50	4.82	1.8
TOTAL INVESTMENTS AND CASH	100.00	100.00	100.00

* Includes bonds of the United States Government, municipalities, utilities, industrial corporations, railroads, and others.

INFLATION AND THE SAVER

Since 1940 the general cost of living in this country has gone up about 73 per cent. Among the causes are the upward spiral of wages and our huge shipments overseas both during and after the war. The basic factor in the inflation, however, is the enormously expanded money supply now in circulation. This great expansion in our money supply, as we saw in the banking chapter, was the direct outcome of the lodging of billions of dollars of federal debt in our commercial banking system during the war and immediately after.

Inflation hurts the saver in two ways. First, it shrinks the purchasing power of accumulated savings. With living costs up 73 per cent since 1940, the widow who draws on past savings to finance her current living expenses must now pay $1.73 for things which cost $1.00 in 1940. Many a family head who saved during the war to buy a new home now finds that rising prices have put that home still far beyond his reach. So it is with all Americans who have accumulated savings—they are being swindled by every upward movement of prices. Those who bought savings bonds during and after the war at the urgent solicitation of the Government are among the victims.

A second way inflation hurts the saver is in cutting down sharply the capacity to save. For those with "sticky" incomes—fixed incomes, that is, which failed to keep pace with rising living costs—every upward whirl of prices during the past few years cut into the margin they had hitherto reserved for savings. Many even had to draw on past savings to meet current living expenses. Such inroads on savings are a severe blow to our social structure. They have seriously affected the great middle class—that large segment of the American people with relatively inflexible incomes and which in normal times comprises the backbone of our savers.

Just as the public's money supply was expanded by the sale of government bonds to commercial banks during the war, so it may now be reduced, and inflationary pressures eased, by use of Treasury surpluses to retire federal short-term debt held by the banking system. This was done, in fact, to the extent of several billion dollars during the fiscal year 1948 and it was a wise step. The Treasury can also pay off debt held by the banks by selling bonds to non-bank investors. This was the primary purpose of the long-term government bond sale to non-bank investors in the fall of 1947. Both these measures are important moves in the fight against inflation. They should be repeated vigorously as long as strong inflationary pressures persist.

FEDERAL TAXATION AND THE SAVER

At present government revenue runs about 40 billion dollars. This is an enormous peacetime burden on the taxpayer; nevertheless, as long as inflationary forces remain strong, wise fiscal policy requires a budgetary surplus. Every effort must be made to reduce federal expenditures. By this means, the great weight of taxes can be lightened without weakening the fight against inflation.

Federal taxation bears down heavily on all savers, up and down the income scale. Drastic reduction in personal income tax exemptions during the war, together with the sharp rise in prices, made it virtually impossible for those whose status remained unchanged in the lower and middle income brackets to save. Many of them had to draw on past savings and borrow. A beginning was made in tax reduction in the spring of 1948, but today new spending proposals are threatening higher taxes.

For those trying to better their incomes and build up an estate, steeply progressive surtax rates are depressing obstacles. How the tax collector siphons off income is shown in the section on "Restrictive Effect of Taxes" in Chapter 2. Even after the 1948 tax reductions, a married man with no dependents receiving $2,500 net income, works for the Government one day out of every fifteen. If he is industrious and successful and increases his net earnings to $10,000, he works for the Government one-seventh of his time. At $25,000 the proportion is one-fifth, and at $50,000 it is between one-fourth and one-third. Should this man reach a net income of $100,000, he would be working for the Government five months of every year.

Tax rates, graduated in this fashion, place an onerous burden on those who normally would save and invest their funds in venturesome enterprise. More and more economists now agree that the almost confiscatory tax rates as one climbs the income ladder weaken the ability to save, hold back investment in new industry, and heavily penalize initiative.

At practically all income levels present taxes take their toll of saving and investment. In the interest of a healthy peacetime economy, the weight of taxes on the saving and investment process should be reduced.

LOW INTEREST RATES AND SAVINGS

Still another burden is placed on savers. When the worldwide depression came in the thirties, governments all over the globe adopted monetary policies designed to reduce interest rates. The object was to facilitate government deficit financing and stimulate business recovery by making it easy to borrow. Chapter 4 describes the effects of our government's low-interest policy, how it precipitated a further decline in rates late in the war and after.

It is now generally agreed that further reductions would not encourage investment and that they are not needed. It is also recognized that lower rates can be maintained only by forces which expand the money supply and increase inflation.

One encouraging sign was in the spring of 1946, when the Treasury and Federal Reserve began to move slowly away from freezing interest rates at excessively low wartime levels. An increasing awareness of government officials to the danger in falling rates was expressed a year later to the House

Banking and Currency Committee by Marriner S. Eccles, then chairman of the Board of Governors of the Federal Reserve System.

"It would be undesirable," said Mr. Eccles, "particularly in a period of inflationary pressures, to have long-term interest rates forced down through monetization of the [federal] debt. A decline in long-term interest rates resulting from an excess of savings over the demand for investment funds would be desirable, but a decline because of bank credit expansion would be undesirable. Such a development would be an inflationary influence; it would also reduce the return on savings and, therefore, impose a serious burden on individuals and institutions, such as insurance companies, schools and benevolent societies, that are dependent on interest returns for their incomes. Should long-term rates decline much lower, many of the functions performed by these institutions would have to be taken over by government, thus leading in the direction of socialism."

Here is a careful expression of the changes involved in a government action which penalizes savings and weakens savings institutions. Since the wartime bulge the rate of saving has materially declined. It remains to be seen whether the current rate is adequate for the growing capital requirements of the country. Already for some types of capital—particularly risk capital for new and expanding enterprise—the flow of savings has been seriously restricted by multiple burdens placed on those who supply this capital. And an easing of these burdens should be one objective of the government's fiscal policy.

SUMMARY

1. The phenomenal growth in America's industrial power and improvement in American living standards is due in large measure to saving and to productive use of savings in investment in factories, railroads, utilities, homes, and schools.

2. While nearly everyone saves, the bulk of the individual saving is done by families with incomes over $5,000. To an increasing extent American savers have channeled their funds through institutions such as life insurance companies, banks, building and loan associations, and trust companies, which put savings to work in our industrial system. Business concerns also save part of their earnings to finance capital requirements.

3. Notwithstanding the vital part that savings have played in this country's development, and the fact that they are still sorely needed for further economic progress, certain government policies have tended in recent years to discourage saving: (a) inflation has cut down many persons' ability to save and has deprived others of much of the value of their savings, (b) taxes weigh heavily on the incentive to save and invest, and (c) excessively low interest rates weaken the inducement to save.

4. To correct these dangerous tendencies, we need a fiscal and monetary policy that will avoid an inflationary expansion of the money supply; we need a reduction in the tax burden on saving and investment, and greater flexibility of interest rates.

6

THE DEBT AND LIFE INSURANCE

THREE out of every four American families own life insurance. Millions of other people in all walks of life are beneficiaries of life insurance and depend upon it for some or all of their support. The relationship between the national debt and life insurance therefore affects the majority of our population.

For another reason apart from this, the influence of the national debt on life insurance is of great importance to the country as a whole. As is brought out in the preceding chapter, life insurance is a form of saving. Through life insurance companies, more than 75 million persons had accumulated by the end of 1947 about 44 billion dollars in savings, or 40 per cent of total personal savings placed with institutions. Clearly, the investment of this large volume of savings by life insurance companies plays a significant role in the Nation's economy. It provides means for the steady upward march in the Nation's standard of living.

DEBT AND THE POLICYHOLDER

In the wartime expansion of the national debt to 279 billions, life insurance companies became one of the best, most reliable customers of the U. S. Treasury. Even though they have sold some of their bonds since then, they still are the largest holders—more than 30 per cent—of the Treasury's long-term bonds. Over 30 per cent of life insurance assets are government securities. Thus the interest which the Government pays on its securities affects the income of life insurance companies. Beyond that, the Government's rate policy affects the interest rates the companies receive from their other investments. This has an impact on the cost of carrying insurance.

Probably an even more important link is that the purchasing power of the dollars paid to beneficiaries is influenced by the prudence with which the Nation's fiscal affairs are managed. It makes a difference to every policyholder whether the Government's fiscal program inflates or deflates the volume, and conversely the value, of dollars. Hence life-insurance beneficiaries have a direct stake in such things as balancing the budget, increase or decrease in the debt, and how much national debt is owned by commercial banks and the Federal Reserve System as contrasted with other types of investors; for all these matters affect the purchasing power of the insurance dollar.

Much of the effect war-bred inflation had on life insurance beneficiaries was probably unavoidable; it was part of the price that society paid for a great war. But the dilemmas created by a large national debt remain and call for wise and statesmanlike debt management. In such management, the Government will, of course, consider various aspects of the public welfare. Not the least of these is the effect of debt and fiscal decisions upon life insurance and its beneficiaries. Government policies will reflect the people's understanding of these questions and their willingness to support wise and far-sighted action.

LIFE INSURANCE AND THE INDIVIDUAL

To most families the death of the bread-winner is not only a personal, but a financial, tragedy. The primary purpose of life insurance is to keep the financial side of such an unpredictable loss from becoming a catastrophe to the family.

For the average citizen, life insurance is the surest method by which he can provide for his dependents after his death. In other forms of financial accumulation there is risk that death will strike before sufficient funds have been saved and soundly invested. Such a risk is greatly reduced, if not removed, through life insurance.

This is accomplished by a pooling of interest and a sharing of risks. The burdens of those who die prematurely are shared by those who live longer than the average life-time. Without insurance, neither the short-lived nor even the average person has the likelihood or expectation of accumulating much by other savings methods before he dies. Furthermore, income-taxes make the task more difficult than formerly.

SIZE AND LIMITATIONS OF LIFE INSURANCE

Although the purpose of life insurance is well known, it is not so generally realized that there are practical limits to the amount of protection a person can afford. In most cases, for example, it is prohibitively expensive for a man to provide his dependents with as large an income as he had while he was still alive and earning. Life insurance is, therefore, something that replaces *part*, by no means all, of a man's contributions to his family interrupted by death, disability or old age. Even with the help of life insurance, dependents do not generally have nearly so many dollars of income to pay for food, clothing, shelter and other living costs.

The dollars received from life insurance are not usually extra dollars to provide luxuries; they are essential and therefore precious dollars. These insurance dollars can fulfill their purpose only if, through wise management of the national debt, our government protects the purchasing power of the dollar.

How widespread is the desire to protect dependents through life insurance can be seen from a survey of consumer finances made by the Federal Reserve Board in 1947. Payment of life insurance premiums was the most frequent form of savings reported by all income groups. This survey revealed that 78 per cent of all families in the United States owned life insurance in 1946. The percentage was slightly higher in upper income groups and slightly less in lower income ones, but even in the $1,000 to $1,999-income category, 73 per cent of all families carried life insurance. As might be expected, families with dependents more often carry insurance. In urban areas, where workers lack the natural security provided by farm ownership, an even larger percentage of families seek life insurance protection. In metropolitan areas, for example, 86 per cent of the families own some life insurance.

The benefits paid out by life companies are impressively large. In 1947 the total payments to policyholders and beneficiaries were three billion dollars. Of this, nearly 1.3 billions represented death payments, while another 720 millions were paid on matured endowments, on annuities, and for disabilities. These great sums, consisting mainly of money which people provided for themselves and their dependents through voluntary sacrifices, relieve society of a part of the burden of taxing or borrowing for relief purposes.

The size and purpose of this protection prompt two questions: How has our national debt affected life insurance? How is the future handling of this debt likely to affect present and prospective owners of life insurance?

Every policyholder out of the many millions and every beneficiary may be an individual and perhaps highly complicated case. Nevertheless, it is broadly true that the unprecedentedly rapid rise of the national debt since 1940 has set up forces, inflationary and otherwise, which have placed increasingly severe burdens upon those who rely upon life insurance for protection.

Policyholders have special difficulty in adjusting to these burdens because they are growing older, and the cost of *additional* insurance for any one person automatically rises as he grows older. For example, the cost of a new ordinary life policy is about 25 per cent higher when issued to a man of 46 than to a man of 40.

Specifically, policyholders have been subjected to three pressures:

LIFE INSURANCE AND THE COST OF LIVING

1. The cost of living has gone up. This means that a thousand dollars of life insurance buys much less in 1949 than it would have bought in 1941.

The rise in prices pinches those whose spendable income (after tax deductions) has failed to rise proportionately. People who depend upon such fixed incomes as the proceeds of life insurance or annuities, are the most conspicuous victims of this squeeze. Unless they can supplement their incomes, they are deprived, as inflation proceeds, first of luxuries and later of some necessities of life. They receive the same number of dollars, but the dollars do less work.

Typically, insurance beneficiaries are people who because of age, sex, broken health, disability or family responsibility have rigidly limited earning capacities. Their chief protection and income are derived from insurance, and a decline of purchasing power is particularly serious. Once again it should be emphasized that the average citizen can buy out of income only a modest amount of insurance—only enough insurance income to replace *part* of his normal income if interrupted by death or disability.

In 1940, the average man may have thought, justifiably enough, that if he died his family could, with stringent economy, take care of the necessities of life with an income of $100 a month from his life insurance. His old insurance policies still provide $100 a month, but the living that cost only $100 in 1940 now costs $173.

Thus when living costs are higher, more life insurance is needed to give a family adequate protection. This is one reason for the enormous increase in the purchase of new life insurance since the beginning of the war. Many thousands of Americans have struggled to adjust their insurance to the change in living costs. Another reason for increased insurance is higher incomes, especially among wage-earners, coupled with a desire to save.

Despite large increases in volume of life insurance outstanding over the last several years, over-all protection has not kept pace with the cost of living. Diagram 24 shows how the amount of insurance in force per family has fallen behind.

AVAILABLE INCOME FOR INSURANCE

2. Higher living costs and heavier taxes prevent large numbers of people from buying the additional insurance they need. Millions of persons, it is true, have much larger incomes than ever before. Even after allowing for taxes and rise in living costs, many of these incomes are greater in purchasing

power. But millions of other insured families could not increase their protection because they lacked money for it.

The average wage-earner usually has only a narrow margin over and above essential living expenses and taxes. Higher taxes and steeper living costs have eaten heavily into many

DIAGRAM 24

AVERAGE FAMILY'S LIFE INSURANCE AND COST OF LIVING both rose from 1940 but the cost of living rose faster than the amount of insurance.

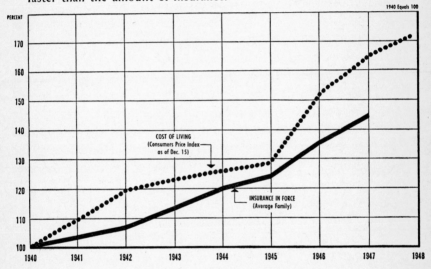

of these margins. Yet it is out of these margins that insurance premiums are paid.

A U. S. Department of Labor study of family spending in 1941 demonstrates the relationship of insurance ownership to earnings and spendings. The typical family of two or more members earning between $2,000 and $3,000 in 1941, had a total cash income of $2,479, out of which it saved $147. If this same family had maintained its standard of living in 1947 and increased its savings so as to afford enough additional life insurance for the same protection as in 1941, its income would have risen from $2,479 to $4,255, or by 72 per cent. The increase would have been still more in 1948, when living costs continued to rise. Many families have lacked any such rise in income.

INTEREST RATES AND INSURANCE COSTS

3. The net cost of insurance has risen because of the Government's policy of extremely low interest rates. The money insurance companies pay out in benefits comes chiefly from two sources—current premium payments and income from earlier premium payments saved up and invested. The level of interest rates determines the yield of by far the largest part of the sums invested, and, as Chapter 4 shows, this level not only on government bonds but on all investments hinges largely on the Government's management of the national debt. Since the early 1930's the Government has maintained interest rates at an unprecedentedly low level.

Declines in the prevailing rate of interest caused the net earnings of a representative group of life insurance companies to drop from about 5.0 per cent in 1930 to 2.9 per cent in 1947. (See Diagram 25.) This reduction of about 40 per cent is really a cut in the wages of securely invested savings. Translating these percentages into dollars, the Life Insurance Association of America has figured that if 1947 investment earnings had been at the same interest rate as in 1930, they would have been $1,045,608,000 more than they were.

Insurance companies have adjusted themselves as best they could to offset this reduction of income. There were ways this could be done, fortunately, though not without cost to policyholders.

Most life insurance in this country is on a "participating basis." At the end of each year a company knows what its

claims and expenses have been, and after reserves required
by law and needed contingencies have been set aside, part
of the premiums are paid back to policyholders as "dividends." In the accepted commercial sense, these are not divi-

DIAGRAM 25

NET EARNINGS OF LIFE INSURANCE COMPANIES ON INVESTMENTS

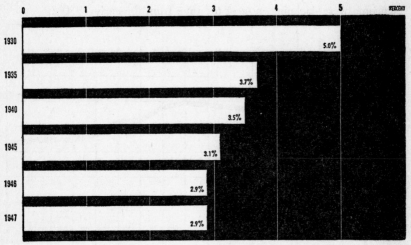

From Life Insurance Association of America—data for 49 companies representing
89.9 per cent of admitted assets of all U. S. companies.

dends but are simply refunds of premiums the companies
found they needed no longer. Put another way, premiums are
set at levels which cover not only the expected cost of insurance but a margin for unforeseen circumstances. If these contingencies do not develop, the margin can be safely returned
to policyholders.

Premium rates for nonparticipating policies are based on
estimates as close as can safely be made of future mortality,
future interest earnings and future expenses. Since the early

1930's there have been some increases in premium rates for new policies sold on the nonparticipating plan, resulting from the decrease in interest earnings on policyholder funds.

Reductions in dividend scales were the most effective method used by participating companies during the past fif-

DIAGRAM 26

DIVIDENDS TO POLICY HOLDERS as a percent of premium income were declining most of the time from the early 1930's.

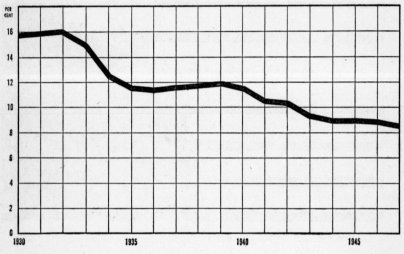

From *Spectator Life Insurance Year Books.*

teen years to offset the drop in investment earnings. Since the early 1930's there has been a progressive downtrend in dividend scales—illustrated in Diagram 26. In 1930, policyholders received back as dividends 15.7 per cent of their premiums, whereas dividends now are less than 8.6 per cent of their premiums. The difference between these two figures represents the added cost of carrying insurance. A rough measure of that difference in 1947 alone was about 475 million dollars. The effect of this increase is felt by every American family carrying life insurance, which is 78 out of every hundred.

Many companies increased their premium rates on new policies. Old policies could not be altered. The combined result has been that the net cost (the premiums less the dividends) of carrying life insurance was somewhere between 10 to 30 per cent higher in 1947 than it was in 1930—depending on the type and plan of policy and the age at which it was issued.

Although alongside of other prices, increased insurance costs may not seem excessive, two points should not be overlooked. One is that the cost of life insurance actually would have declined since 1930 had not the interest rate dropped so low.

A second point is that the greater cost of life insurance cannot be compared fairly with rises in costs of food or ordinary consumer goods. The insurance policyholder accepted a contract for the future delivery of dollars, and dollars are not worth what they were before the war. Yet, by contrast, a pound of meat one buys today contains just as much food value as meat did in 1930. Dollars are not only cheaper in terms of other things, but a dollar's worth of insurance costs more.

These facts should be faced realistically—not only by the armies of policyholders, but by beneficiaries. They are the aftermath of a war which had to be financed regardless of cost, but this debt must not now be managed without regard to consequences.

FUTURE INFLUENCE OF NATIONAL DEBT

As we have seen, our national debt is far larger than it has ever been, not only in dollar volume but even in relation to the expanded national wealth and income. It promises for the indefinite future to exert powerful influence upon business activity, national income and the cost of living. Interest rates established on Treasury securities are also likely to dominate all interest rates, especially those on high-grade corporate securities and mortgages such as life insurance companies buy and hold.

It seems clear that future government decisions about national debt and interest rates will greatly influence life insurance. Probably of first concern to policyholders will be the impact of debt management on the value of their beneficiaries' dollar, that is to say, on the purchasing power of their insurance.

FUTURE OF INTEREST RATES

Hardly less significant to policyholders than the future purchasing power of their insurance dollars is the future earning power of those dollars. What rate of interest will the money which policyholders have entrusted to insurance companies be able to earn without assumption of undue investment risks?

From the standpoint of policyholders, security and life insurance are synonymous. Maintaining this security, therefore, transcends all other responsibilities of life-insurance managements. Their first duty is to see to it that their companies always have sufficient sums to meet all contractual claims.

Contrasted with businesses with quick turnovers, the life insurance business deals mainly with long-term contracts. Today many policies are being written on the lives of children and these may remain in force not only during the lifetimes of the insured, but beyond that, during the lifetimes of their eventual beneficiaries—well into the twenty-first century. Even though economic conditions may change greatly, a life company cannot increase the premiums on a policy, once it is issued. That is why premium levels are set high enough for a margin of safety against the unforeseen.

Two of the most important factors considered in setting premium rates are the probable mortality rate and an assumption as to what interest can be earned on the funds which accumulate while the policies are in force. Here is the nut to crack. If, because of prevailing low interest rates, a life insurance company cannot earn as much on invested funds as it expected when it issued its policies, then it must somehow make up the deficiency from other sources.

It is sometimes said, especially by advocates of a national policy of low interest rates, that such rates are not burdensome because the mortality risks have been greatly reduced. National health has improved, it is true, and the average life span has been increased, but the resulting savings to life companies do not offset the drop in investment earnings. This is one compelling reason why insurance companies have reduced the dividends they return to policyholders; the companies need these funds so as to assure the policyholder's security.

Although some companies can use gains from mortality to offset lower interest earnings, that condition is likely to be temporary; it will tend to disappear as the insurance is outstanding for longer periods. The longer a life insurance policy remains in force, the more funds are built up to its credit and the more important the rate of interest becomes in the determination of income. As interest becomes more important as a source of income, mortality savings become less so for two reasons. First, the amount at risk decreases—that is, the closer the reserves approach the face amount of the policy, the less effect mortality has on the insurance transaction. Second, improvement in mortality rates has been relatively unimportant at older ages—the ages which are involved as the insurance grows older, the funds larger, and the "amount at risk" smaller. For these reasons, mortality savings cannot be counted upon to offset fully the decline in interest earnings.

Government policy of very low interest rates has had another important effect upon life companies. Not only has the yield on current new investments been reduced, but it has been lowered, as a result, upon the non-government securities already in the portfolios of insurance companies. In 1945 and 1946 alone, eight billions of new corporate securities were floated at lower interest rates to refund outstanding issues.

As a result of these refundings, a considerable part of the bonds held by most life insurance companies at the start of 1945 were paid off before they were due—and most were refinanced at lower rates disadvantageous to life insurance.

While interest rates on prime securities stiffened somewhat in late 1947 and in 1948, they benefit life insurance only when new funds are invested at the higher rates of return. They do not increase the investment income from the securities already in insurance portfolios. Even if the interest trend is higher during the next few years, it is unlikely that the investment income of life companies will rise as rapidly as it declined between 1930 and 1946.

ADJUSTING TO THE SITUATION

Whatever the government policy on the control and level of interest rates, it seems clear that life companies will have to cut their cloth to fit the pattern. If the Government continues to favor low interest rates, some difficult decisions must be made. These are background factors:

As mentioned earlier, the interest rate is an important factor in determining premiums. Before the early 1930's, the investment earnings of companies doing 90 per cent of all life business, had always substantially exceeded 4 per cent. In computing premiums, these companies conservatively estimated that earnings of only 3.2 per cent would be enough to build up their insurance reserves by the required legal amounts. Actually, in 1930, they earned 5.0 per cent. In 1947 the average assumption of interest earnings required to maintain the reserves had declined to about 2.9 per cent, but actual

DIAGRAM 27

MARGIN OF ACTUAL INVESTMENT EARNINGS
above those needed to maintain policy reserves shrank from 37.8 percent in 1930 to 3.4 percent in 1947.

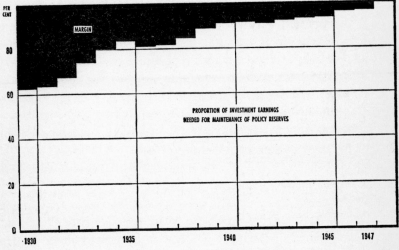

From Mutual Life Insurance Co. of New York, data on twenty large companies.

interest earnings had dropped to nearly as low a rate. The significance is that in 1930, the margin of actual interest earnings was 37.8 per cent above interest earnings needed to maintain reserves, but by 1947 the margin had dropped to 3.4 per cent of actual interest earnings. Diagram 27 portrays the change.

Insurance companies, like bankers, know from long experience that they must be prepared to absorb investment losses. This is because there are always some borrowers who, under adverse economic or local conditions, cannot meet their obligations on their bonds or mortgages. The insurance managements must therefore consider how to build up surpluses during prosperity to cushion their companies against adversity. In sharp contrast to times when interest rates were higher, the current narrow margin of interest earnings over interest requirements does not provide suitably for this purpose.

In spite of this, many insurance companies during the past few years have greatly strengthened their surplus accounts. Much of the funds for this came from the fact that many corporations were willing to pay above par for the privilege of retiring their outstanding securities so that they could issue new ones at lower interest. The amounts above par received were, in reality, only a partial offset to the lower interest which will be paid over a period of years on the new securities issued in exchange. It seems doubtful whether capital gains comparable to those during the recent past will materialize in the years immediately ahead.

LIFE INSURANCE AND THE U. S. TREASURY

It has been shown that the future earnings of life insurance companies on their investments will depend much if not largely upon the Treasury's interest-rate and debt-management policies. The shoe also fits the other foot: life insurance investment is and will continue to be of great importance to the Treasury.

Life companies in the United States hold about 17 billion dollars of government securities. These holdings are primarily long-term obligations, for which the companies are probably the Treasury's best customer. This is important to the Treasury, because such bonds present no problems of early maturity or need for refunding. Life companies com-

posed the largest single group of purchasers of the long-term
2½ per cent bonds issued during the Defense, War Loan and
Victory drives. Diagram 28 shows how they and other investors accumulated these securities during the war years.

DIAGRAM 28

LIFE INSURANCE COMPANY HOLDINGS of Treasury's long-term 2½ percent bonds have been the largest of any class of investors.

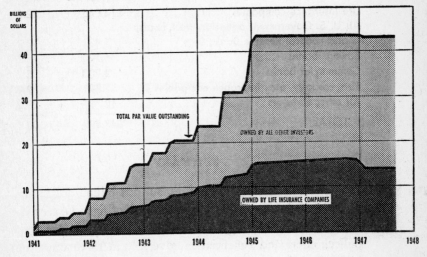

From U. S. Treasury Bulletins.

Ownership of these issues as of August 31, 1948, was distributed as in Table 9 (page 136).

Life insurance companies have a steady flow of new investment funds which are now over 3½ billions a year. Depending on other demands and provided the interest return meets
life insurance earning requirements, the companies are likely
to be sizable investors in Treasury securities for a long time.
Moreover, their purchases are non-inflationary—they do not
lead to an increase in the money supply. As long-term in-

vestors, therefore, life insurance companies can play an im
portant part in the future financing of the national debt.

TABLE 9

RECENT HOLDINGS OF LONG-TERM TREASURY 2½ PER CENT BONDS

(Dollar amounts in millions)

	Aug. 31, 1948	Per Cent
Life insurance companies	$14,045	32.2
All U. S. Government agencies, trust funds, and Federal Reserve Banks	7,452	17.2
Savings banks	6,190	14.2
Commercial banks	2,283	5.2
Fire, casualty, etc., insurance companies	891	2.0
All other investors	12,737	29.2
TOTAL	$43,598	100.0

SUMMARY

1. For most American families, our 201 billion-dollar total
of life insurance provides the cornerstone of financial security.

2. Forces set up by wartime finance have affected these
policyholders and beneficiaries adversely in three ways: (a)
higher living costs have lowered the purchasing power of insurance protection, (b) higher taxes and living costs have
made it harder for many people to save and purchase life
insurance, and (c) at a time when more insurance is needed,
lower interest rates have made it more costly because of reduced earnings on insurance company investments.

3. To insurance policyholders, along with other groups of
the population, it is important, therefore, that debt management have as a major objective the preservation of the value
of the dollar. It should work towards economic stability, not

towards inflation or deflation. Also, in its interest-rate policy it should consider the saver as well as the borrower of money.

4. Because life insurance companies are the largest owners of the Treasury's long-term securities, with a large and steady supply of incoming funds for long-term investment, they can play an important part in future financing of the national debt.

7

WHAT TO DO ABOUT IT

WE have seen how a towering national debt of 250 billion dollars affects our money supply, our interest rates, our savings and the life insurance policies of three out of every four American families. We have seen how expanding national wealth and productivity helped to reduce the debts arising from previous wars. We have also seen how excessive bank holdings of government securities have helped to inflate the money supply; and how low interest and high tax rates have discouraged savings needed for investment in an expanding economy so necessary for reduction of the national debt.

It is therefore plain that the American people should be seriously concerned about their Nation's debt. The problem is how to make that concern effective, how we can live safely with this gigantic obligation, with a minimum of hardship and the least drain on the vitality of our economy. We must be realistic enough to face our fears, size up our dangers, and decide what can be done to avert them.

WHAT WE HAVE TO FEAR

Some of our fears are extravagant, and what may seem to be lesser dangers are the most perilous. A few persons fear that the debt may cause some vast, vague cataclysm, that it may topple over and crush them. They wonder whether the Treasury can sell enough securities to meet the 40 billions plus of debt which matures within a year. They worry lest the market for Treasury issues should dry up and force the Government into default. They remember the repudiation in 1933 of the gold clause in the Nation's obligations and they fear the possibility that sometime the Government might be unable or unwilling to meet its obligations when they fall due, that the Government might repudiate its national debt and go into some form of bankruptcy.

Such dread is natural. People worry likewise about their own debts. A personal debt can be like a millstone about one's neck—even bring about such disasters as loss of a home when mortgage payments cannot be met. With a national debt amounting to about $6,300 for each family, a sum nearly twice the average family annual income, no wonder some people are fearful. But although a national debt can be more serious than a private one, its impact on people is different.

Without a political revolution, it is hardly likely that the United States Government would resort to outright debt repudiation. Strong stigma would attach to anyone proposing it or daring to vote for it. Also, repudiation would create more problems than it would solve. Since banks, insurance companies, trust funds and the like hold large chunks of the debt, the Government either would have to compensate them for their losses, or allow the economy to become completely paralyzed. Besides, there would be no need for the Government to repudiate outright; there are more indirect ways.

Unlike persons, governments can raise money for their debts by taxation, although, of course, excessive use of this power slowly stifles the energies of the people and in the end means less tax revenue. But even if their tax revenues aren't enough to meet debt charges, nations would not have to default on their obligations. They have two other expedients. They can create more money, either by the printing press or bank credit, and thus pay off debts in inflated currency of lower purchasing power. Or they can place conditions on the rights of owners of government securities to redeem their holdings at maturity or to trade them freely in open markets. Actually, both expedients amount to partial repudiation, but they are not always recognized as such.

And so, sudden catastrophe is not the real danger surrounding our national debt. The biggest perils are more subtle, and they are four.

1. The dilution of the dollar.
2. The risk of boom and bust.
3. The smothering of enterprise.
4. The loss of human freedoms.

1. DILUTION OF THE DOLLAR

During the war, vast expenditures diluted the dollar. Currency and bank deposits increased much faster than the country's production and volume of business. Since then labor union pressure forced up wages. Government subsidies and price supports for farmers helped to keep food costs high. Huge shipments for foreign relief cut down our own supplies of necessities and raised their prices. Easy mortgage credit put more money in circulation. With more people eager to buy more things than are available to sell, price competition has not been normal.

All these were powerful inflationary forces. We have more dollars than before, but they don't buy as much as they once did.

We were moderately successful during the war in holding inflation in check. This was partly because of rationing and price controls. It would have been impossible without the good sense of the American people, most of whom were willing to save much of their increased accumulations of dollars and refused to buy scarce goods at consistently higher prices. But when we turned from war to peace, and wartime restraints were lifted, it was clear that we had not cured inflation but had merely arrested it; we still had inflation. The wage-price spiral soared until, in 1948, prices slightly exceeded the post-World War I peak of 1920 as shown in Diagram 1 on page 5.

No one can predict the price movement from month to month, but this much can be said from experience—the further the inflation goes the greater will be the danger of deflation and depression when the turn comes. A great underlying cause has been the vastly increased money supply—the diluted dollar working with the other factors mentioned above.

To Deflate or Not to Deflate?

Much can be said for a price level permanently higher than prewar as an aid for carrying our huge debt. The more dollars farmers, wage-earners and businessmen get for their products and services, the easier for them to pay the heavy taxes needed for debt service and other government costs. Already there has been much economic adjustment to higher prices. By and large, wages and salaries have advanced. People have incurred new debts for homes and other purchases. Industry has invested billions of present-day dollars in new plant and equipment on which it hopes to get a return.

Once these adjustments have been made, they cannot easily be unmade. Wages once raised cannot readily be reduced. Nor can debts be painlessly adjusted downward except over long periods. Thus, a return to prewar prices would mean another violent wrench to our economy. It would mean widespread unemployment, mortgage foreclosures, business failures and the general distress of 1920-21 and of the early thirties. Such deflation to cure inflation is like running over a man with an automobile, then, to make amends, backing up over him again.

DIAGRAM 29

PURCHASING POWER OF THE CONSUMER'S DOLLAR
shows the effect of inflation in sinking to a new low since 1914.

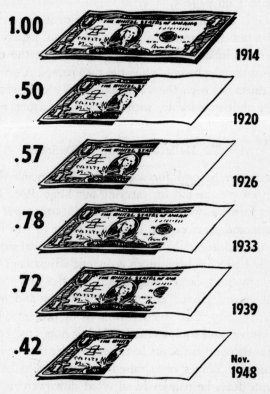

1.00   1914

.50   1920

.57   1926

.78   1933

.72   1939

.42   Nov. 1948

There is another side of the picture. The change in value of the dollar in terms of retail prices, housing and other general items since 1914 is shown in Diagram 29. We have seen in Chapter 5 how wartime and postwar inflation wiped out a considerable portion of the value of savings bank deposits, life insurance and savings bonds. The standard of living of persons with fixed incomes was reduced in many cases to actual hardship. We all know the plight of churches, hospitals, colleges and charitable institutions: on one hand largely dependent on fixed-income investments; on the other, squeezed by rising costs and falling interest rates. All these gross inequities threaten the independence of privately financed organizations and discourage savings needed for economic development.

In short, inflation has brought about a reshuffling of national wealth and income. Some groups have benefited at the expense of others. To reconcile these conflicting human interests would tax the wisdom of Solomon. It would call for arbitrary action far outside the workings of our democratic principles. It cannot be done by overhead authority, but must be allowed to work itself out through the interplay of changing conditions of supply and demand, productive efficiency, and other factors that enter into establishing a price relationship that *works* and that encourages a maximum exchange of goods and services in the economy.

While attaining this new equilibrium, some prices which have lagged heretofore may "catch up." Others which went ahead too fast will undergo correction, as did the 1948 grain prices. All in all, it would probably be easier and less disruptive to high production of physical wealth and services if adjustments both ways are made to a general level that involves neither further price inflation nor deep deflation.

However, the gravest danger with a diluted dollar is a renewed inflationary eruption whenever the people's mood is buoyant. Again we say, the greater the inflation the more severe will be the ultimate reaction. The most important policy today is to avoid further inflation.

2. THE RISK OF BOOM AND BUST

A big debt accentuates economic instability by interference with sound government monetary and fiscal policies. As long as the Government has so huge a problem of financing, the temptation is great to freeze interest rates very low. As we have seen, this freezing threatens economic stability in two ways:

First, the process of pegging markets to keep down interest rates is inflationary. Unless action is offset in other ways, the government support of government securities prices adds to the money supply—which is directly inflationary.

Second, freezing of interest rates interferes with credit controls by central banks which involve changes in interest rates. Though far from perfect, these controls have been for many years the chief method in this and other countries for avoiding the disastrous pattern of boom and bust.

Other devices have been suggested for holding down fluctuations of the business cycle—notably the "compensatory" budget expounded by the British economic philosopher, John Maynard Keynes. As Chapters 2 and 5, which discuss the Keynes doctrine, bring out, neither this nor any other proposed substitute for credit control has yet passed the test of experience.

It would be folly to throw overboard credit control which has repeatedly shown its value, until we have found a better one. Frozen interest rates imperil business stability; with them there is greater risk of booms and depressions.

3. THE SMOTHERING OF ENTERPRISE

The national debt saps the vitality of our economic life. In private life excessive debt is like a leech which sucks off the strength of the debtor; so in public life a high national debt has a constant debilitating effect in two ways:

(a) The drain of taxes.

(b) Excessive government controls.

From personal experience all of us know much about these two dangers. We know how taxes deter business concerns and individuals from greater effort. We know how they hold back the growth of the country. The best single long-term offset to the debt burden is a high and expanding economic activity that will provide the means to lift it. High taxes smother and retard.

As to (b), recent years have shown how a huge and growing national debt brings more government controls into our economic life. Dilution of the dollar and inflationary debt financing provoke demands for price controls, rent controls, wage controls, and the like. We are told that because of the debt we must keep interest rates low so as to pay off the debt, and that there must be tighter regulation of the banking system. We know, too, that the bigger the national debt, the harder it is to reduce taxes. Yet the higher the taxes the less able our private economy is to reduce the debt and the more government is called upon to regulate our lives and the dead hand of bureaucracy is laid upon business and enterprise.

4. THE LOSS OF HUMAN FREEDOMS

All this points to the fourth menace of the debt. Like a cancer it grows without our realizing what is happening until too late.

It is often said that because we can "afford" to borrow and spend vast sums in war, we can "afford" to borrow and spend for this or that favored project in peace. Of course, we can do so in the sense of merely being able to provide the money. Mechanisms of the money market and the banking system, or as a last resort the printing presses of the Treasury, can see to that. The real test of what we can afford is what happens to our economic system and to democracy. How much inflation must we suffer? What new tax burdens? How many more government controls? Finally, what does it all add up to in the kind of economy we are going to have? Is it to be one in which people are free to manage their own lives, to strive and to enjoy the fruits of striving? Or one dead level managed by the State?

In short, the price of too much debt is more than dollars and cents. What we do about debt management and the budget is an indication whether we shall resist the trend towards state control and collectivism over so much of the world.

A PROGRAM OF DEBT MANAGEMENT

To avert the four dangers just discussed, this country must have a clear-cut policy for debt management. The program should have two objects, either of which is useless unless the other is realized. One is expert handling of the financial phases of the debt; the other is nourishment of a dynamic, stable national economy. Even if we are technically perfect in handling the debt, the achievement is futile unless the country is financially strong, with a national income capable of the burden of debt service.

We must deal with both the specific problem of the debt and with the broad problem of national well-being. And in the following pages, this Committee presents its program for debt management. It calls for five steps: Control the budget; reduce the debt; distribute the debt; restore flexible interest rates; and nourish a dynamic economy.

1. CONTROL THE BUDGET

The first step is to get the national budget under control. Until we do, all talk of debt "policy" is idle.

Today, nearly four years after the end of the war, we are not sure we have that control. It is true, as Diagram 6 (p. 24) shows, federal expenditures have fallen from their 100 billion-a-year peak, but they are still monumental. As noted in Chapter 2 and its accompanying Table 1, there are huge increases in costs in all but two federal budget non-military classifications.

Under these budgets, the Federal Government receives and spends close to one-fifth of our expanded national income. Add State and local governmental taxes; the fraction is about one-fourth. One dollar out of every four of the people's income goes to central or local government in taxes. Diagram 30 (page 148) shows how this ratio has risen over thirty years. While the ratio declined in 1946 and 1947, this was due not so much to reduction in tax collections as to inflation of national income measured in cheaper dollars. No precise formula can determine the capacity of any people to carry a tax load and still remain prosperous and free. But a ratio of taxes to income as high as 25 per cent is in the danger zone.

The country, moreover, has been going through a business boom, with national income three times as high as before the war. This boom is supported by a huge accumulation of readily available funds as a result of war financing, also by a large deferred demand for houses, machinery, and all types of durable consumption goods.

This combination together with high tax rates produced the tremendous flow of revenue that has more than balanced our huge postwar budgets. We cannot expect the boom to last indefinitely. A budget, therefore, that is balanced only

DIAGRAM 30

NATIONAL INCOME AND TOTAL TAX RECEIPTS
have expanded several-fold since World War I

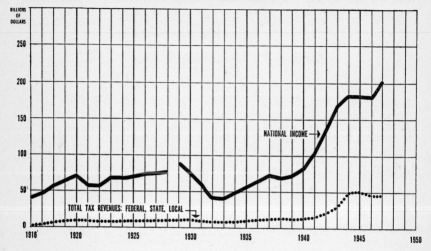

but the RATIO OF TAX REVENUES TO NATIONAL
INCOME reveals the long-term upward trend in the tax burden

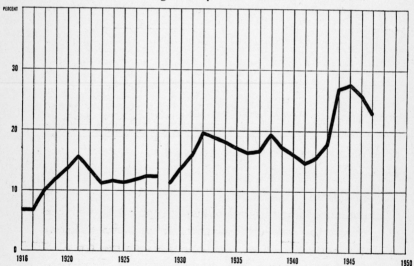

Gaps in the curves are due to a shift from the use of National Industrial Conference Board data on national income, to Department of Commerce data.

at the top of a boom and at a level of taxes that places a serious burden on all the people and on all business, is clearly too big and is a grave risk to the country's welfare.

Arms and Foreign Aid Costs

Instead of continuing downward from swollen wartime levels, federal expenditures now are rising again. Whether we like it or not, events have thrust the United States into world leadership. Millions of people look to us not only to repair the ravages of war, but as guardians of the peace and as a barrier against the spread of militant communism. Congress by a large majority voted more than five billions for the first period of the European Recovery Program. It also made additional appropriations for strengthening the armed forces. Both outlays, which bulk large in the federal budget, were supported by public opinion; and they reflect the American people's awareness of their world-wide responsibilities. Our people know that the safety and welfare of the Nation rest on both marshaling our own resources and the rekindling of the hope and vitality of freedom-loving peoples throughout the world.

Granted that the American people agree upon these objectives, there is still to determine how much money to appropriate and how it can be put to most effective use. Another element is what our already tight employment and materials situation can safely and effectively provide. As Secretary of Defense Forrestal testified before a Congressional committee:

"Careful study must be given to the point at which the impact of additional military procurement, whether it is for the Army, the Air Force or the Navy, added to the demands upon an already practically fully employed and tight economy, may produce explosive inflationary consequences. . . . Dollars alone do not guarantee the delivery of military end products. The military demands must be within the limits of our capacity to produce, or, alternately, we must accept those controls that are found necessary to channel manpower and material necessary to insure the desired production."

No good American wants business-as-usual placed ahead of national security. Yet, short of imminent war, clearly there are limits beyond which it is unwise to push the rate of military procurement. Secretary Forrestal, in testimony to Congress, warned against stocking up on machines already on their way to obsolescence, and quoted an English statesman, "If you left it to the military they'd fortify the moon."

Effectiveness of military spending depends very largely on how much co-ordination exists between the Army, Navy, and Air Force. Real unification of the armed services as Congress envisioned when setting up a single department of national defense has been slow. This was shown by the conflicting testimony of the defense chiefs before the Congress last spring, and by reports of two government boards—the President's Air Policy Commission and the Congressional Aviation Board—and of a subcommittee of the Hoover Commission on Organization of the Executive Branch of the Government. The boards severely criticized the lack of progress in unification, with consequent wastage of money and resources. The subcommittee of the Hoover commission, Ferdinand Eberstadt, chairman, said that unification has not provided the strong central authority necessary to prevent inefficiency, waste and inter-service rivalries. In addition, the Eberstadt subcommittee recommended an overhauling of budget-making in "the world's biggest business," a co-ordination of scientific work with strategic planning and an adequate provision for developing and meeting new methods of warfare.

Costs of national defense are not foreordained. They are matters of policy, planning, and execution, hence adjustable according to how we conceive and carry out our program. Success depends not just on how much we spend, but also on how wisely.

The same is true of economic aid to foreign countries. Too much money, instead of speeding the return of other countries to a self-sustaining basis, can actually increase and prolong their dependence upon us. As the President's Committee on Foreign Aid (the so-called Harriman Committee) stated in its report in November, 1947, "the success of any aid program depends ultimately on hard work and straight thinking by the people and the governments of the European nations themselves. . . . Such aid [as we can give] must be viewed not as a means of supporting Europe, but as a spark which can fire the engine." Consistent with this principle, the President's committee envisioned a steady year-by-year decrease in aid to be given.

Other Economies Essential

At a time like this, when national defense and international aid take so much, every effort should be exerted to keep down federal spending in other directions. Our vast current budgets offer great opportunities for economy if only government and the public are so minded.

Consider veterans' pensions and readjustment benefits which have been costing more than six billion dollars a year, and which in fiscal 1950—five years after the war—are expected still to be as high as $5\frac{1}{2}$ billions. Millions of veterans have been helped to better themselves and take useful places in the community. On the whole, this program has accomplished great good.

It also afforded opportunities and temptations for abuse.

A minority of veterans sat back and drew unemployment compensation rather than take jobs. Educational and on-the-job training programs costing more than two billions annually were described by the President as "being used in some cases to provide training for avocational or leisure time activity at high cost to the Government and without commensurate benefit to veterans." In a veterans' hospitalization and medical aid program costing over one billion in the fiscal year 1949, two-thirds of the veterans are treated for non-service connected disabilities. Too liberal appraisals and credit terms in veterans' housing have helped to inflate realty valuations and building costs. They have boomeranged on veteran home-buyers and may involve both veterans and the Government in losses when the inevitable reaction sets in.

Other heavy outlays call for re-examination. Approximately two billions is budgeted for social welfare projects in the fiscal year 1949. These do not include projects financed by social security taxes, and include only the initial expenses of certain proposed new projects which ultimately might cost billions. Expenditures for civil public works were estimated at 2½ billions for the fiscal year 1949, a new high record, with a further increase of 22 per cent scheduled for 1950.

Aids to agriculture of 1.7 billion in fiscal 1950 include government purchases to support prices at a time when we are supposed to be fighting the high cost of living. Yet, according to the President, American agriculture "is in the best financial condition in history." A subcommittee of the Hoover commission under the chairmanship of Dean H. P. Rusk, of the College of Agriculture, University of Illinois, recommended a major reorganization of the Departments of Agriculture and Interior to eliminate "conflicting, confusing and duplicating" activities. The subcommittee estimated that nearly 100 millions a year might be saved by correcting present operations.

Improve Quality of Government

Various other committees have recommended savings that might be realized through improved administration of federal departments and agencies. Reports were made to the Eightieth Congress by the Joint Congressional Committee on Reduction of Nonessential Federal Expenditures, headed by Senator Byrd; the Joint Congressional Committee on Internal Revenue Taxation, headed by Senator Milliken; the Appropriations Committees of the Senate and House, headed by Senator Bridges and Representative Taber, respectively; and others.

These reports commend and censure government administration. Tribute is paid to devoted service by federal employees, often at low pay and working long hours, frequently with inadequate equipment. Also disclosed are inefficiency and waste which cost taxpayers hundreds of millions of dollars.

These deficiencies partly reflect the laxness that tends to pervade all government bureaucracies. It is partly the result of the tremendous expansion that most government offices have undergone during and since the war. They had hardly a chance to "shake down" and the complicated mechanism got beyond control of top officers of government. Also, it is partly the result of statutory limitations. Department and bureau heads are limited in authority to hire and fire, order new equipment, pay salaries adequate to attract competent people, and to exercise other prerogatives of management.

A report by a subcommittee of the Senate Appropriations Committee of the Eightieth Congress on the workings of the sick and annual leave provisions of the Government is a case in point. Federal employees are entitled to twenty-six days annual leave and fifteen days sick leave each year with full pay. On the basis of the Government's system of counting only working days off as leave (omitting Saturdays and Sundays) they actually get what in private industry would be five and one-fifth weeks annual leave plus three weeks sick leave each year. Both sick leave and annual leave are allowed to accumulate, and all is available to employees after one year of service. Few of the taxpayers who foot these bills do as well.

Examples like these show how our vast and overgrown government structure cries out for re-examination and streamlining. The preliminary reports of the Hoover commission have pointed the way to substantial economies through improvements in administrative organization and methods. It was estimated that, even assuming the continuation of all present governmental functions, annual savings of three billions could be effected.

To have economical government we must have able administrators. This is important not only because of the saving of money, but also because of the tremendously enlarged area of government responsibility and its ever-widening impact on our lives. Experienced observers in government have pointed out that a corps of top-grade administrators is partly a matter of adequate compensation and partly one of allowing executive departments some discretion in making necessary exceptions to routine regulations in the selection and promotion of the best available talent.

What Philosophy of Government?

No matter how successful efforts are to get more efficient performance, the thousand and one functions now asked of government will keep our big budget big. Only by limiting

the number of things we ask government to do, can we hope
to control government spending.

This problem gets down to a philosophy of government.
What do the people expect from the Federal Government?
How much shall be left to individuals, to outside institutions,
to the State and local governments? Education, for example,
has always been a State and local function. The local school
board has been a typically American institution. Now we
hear much of the responsibility of the Federal Government
in these matters. Pressure grows to shift more and more of
the financial load to the Treasury in Washington. Thus does
"big government" grow bigger. Inevitably "big government" means big spending.

Big government means big taxing, with the smothering of
enterprise. It means also a further substitution of government
planning and doing for what the people plan and do for
themselves. Some of this extension of government authority
has been unavoidable as our society has become more complex. It has crept up on us step by step almost without our
realizing it. Much of it was not necessary, but developed
because of the instinct, too common in all classes, to run to
government at the first sign of a difficult problem. And this
instinct has been exploited by certain small but active groups
who want to change the nature of our government.

To cut down and keep down government spending requires
a philosophy of limiting the scope of federal power, as envisioned by the framers of the American Constitution. Unless we have such a philosophy, the tendency is to add one
function after another. Thus the budget grows bigger and
bigger, which not only makes national debt management
vastly more difficult, but leads us far afield from the individual liberty and democracy on which this country has been
built. Thomas Jefferson must have had this danger in mind

when he said, "I am not a friend to a very energetic government. It is always oppressive."

2. REDUCE THE DEBT

After getting the budget under control, the next question is, what about debt retirement?

Just how much the debt should be reduced each year and what statutory requirement should be adopted were discussed in Chapter 2. There is still on the books a law passed in 1919 that the debt should be reduced by a formula in relation to the top figure reached in 1920. The rate of retirement after World War I was several times this legal amount. Since 1931 appropriations have been made each year for this sinking fund, but this has been pure formality, for the debt has risen hugely.

Political pressure for spending and tax reduction is so great that much can be said for setting up a fixed statutory requirement for debt retirement. As pointed out in Chapter 2, the amount of debt retirement should be related to the prosperity of the country, and in a good year we ought to retire more debt than in a bad one. Heavy retirement of debt in prosperous times would be a check to overexpansion and inflationary tendencies. Contrariwise, a smaller retirement, or even a temporary suspension of retirement, in times of adversity, would relieve some of the burden of taxation and would help the processes of recovery.

Under any standards we ought to make a good beginning at debt retirement in times of boom prosperity. Indeed, we have done so. From the peak of 279 billion dollars reached in February, 1946, the total debt by April, 1948, had been reduced to 252 billions, or a decrease of 27 billions over a period of twenty-six months. The debt then remained almost the same for the rest of 1948. Of this debt reduction, 20 billions occurred in 1946 and represented largely the use of excess Treasury balances built up by the Victory Loan in late 1945. Inasmuch as these cash balances were being held idly in the banks, their use to redeem debt was, we have seen, not actually deflationary, but merely removed an inflation potential.

Contrasted with 1946, the debt retirement in 1947 and the early part of 1948, amounting to seven billion, was financed by an excess of receipts over expenditures in the federal budget. The money obtained from taxpayers was used largely to retire debt held by the commercial banking system and thus had a positively deflationary influence which was especially salutary at a time when private borrowing was increasing.

We have made a good start; we must keep it up.

3. DISTRIBUTE THE DEBT

Diagram 31 (page 158) shows what proportion of the federal debt is owned by each group of principal holders. The biggest slice of all—86 billion dollars, or 34 per cent of the total—is held by the commercial banks and Federal Reserve Banks.

National debt is most dangerous when held by banks, for in this form it adds to the money supply. The money supply can be a major inflationary factor. If it expands faster than goods, prices generally go up. So, besides making every effort to reduce the debt's size, it is sound fiscal policy to distribute as much as possible of the present bank-held debt among non-bank investors, who will hold it securely out of the stream of current spending.

This reason is behind the Treasury's wartime policy of selling bonds as widely as it could to individuals, corporations, and institutions other than banks. Even before the war the sound policy was adopted of offering a savings bond that would be attractive to individuals of both large and small means, and selling these bonds to as many people as possible. Savings bonds have been a popular investment; over 75 million persons have bought 55 billion dollars' worth.

DIAGRAM 31

OWNERSHIP OF NATIONAL DEBT.* More than one-third is held by commercial banks and Federal Reserve.

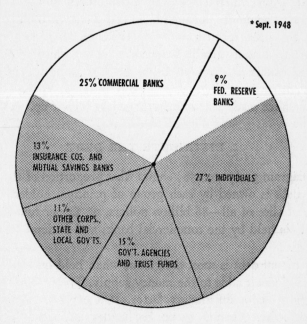

* Sept. 1948

25% COMMERCIAL BANKS

9% FED. RESERVE BANKS

13% INSURANCE COS. AND MUTUAL SAVINGS BANKS

27% INDIVIDUALS

11% OTHER CORPS., STATE AND LOCAL GOV'TS.

15% GOV'T. AGENCIES AND TRUST FUNDS

There are also excellent psychological reasons for wide distribution of the Nation's debt. Public sale of bonds emphasized patriotic support of the war and gave buyers a greater sense of participation. As a result, the United States now has 75 million "shareholders," more people than ever before with a personal stake in affairs of government and particularly in sound financial policies. This can have great bearing on the difficult job of getting and keeping the budget under control. For government spending is not something for which Congress, the President and federal departments are alone responsible. It depends on what the voters insist on getting from their government. And the more voters there are who are taxpayers and bondholders, the less chance there is of unwise, excessive government spending.

There is still another persuasive reason why broad ownership of government bonds safeguards the national welfare. Savings bonds are a cushion against such contingencies as unemployment, illness, and old age. Their spending in times of emergency also helps to keep the country's economic life on an even keel.

Continued, energetic sale of savings bonds is as desirable now as it was during the war; and promotion of that sale is one of the best contributions bankers and businessmen can make to wise management of the public debt.

In addition to the sale of savings bonds the Treasury should be constantly alert to the markets for Treasury long-term bonds. As fast as insurance companies, savings banks, trust accounts, and individuals have money which they are willing to put into long-term government bonds it is sound public policy to issue and sell bonds adapted to the needs of various types of investors. A continued wide distribution of such bonds is far more important than the slight rise in interest rates which may be needed to attract investors. To decide this question on the basis solely of interest saving would be narrow and short-sighted.

The wide distribution of the debt is sound because it reduces the volume of inflationary money, reduces the floating debt which has to be refunded from year to year, and puts the country in stronger position to meet future emergencies.

4. RESTORE FLEXIBLE INTEREST RATES

Interest rates have two great functions which cannot be performed unless they have some flexibility. One of these functions is to adjust the supply of savings to the amount which a dynamic economy needs. Apart from the dearth of "equity money," money has indeed been generally plentiful since the war. But this supply has reflected mainly the expansion of bank credit, particularly that which took place during the war. In the long run the price of money—the interest rate—must be attractive to insure a flow of needed savings.

The restrictive effect of fixed rates on the supply of money is today being illustrated in the 4 per cent rate now set by the Veterans' Administration for G. I. mortgages. The rate is unattractive and the supply of such money is rapidly drying up; so it is hard for veterans to get mortgage money. It is the old law of supply and demand at work.

The second and more immediate function of interest rates is control of the flow of credit. Booms in the old days were checked when the money ran out, and a rise in money rates was a signal of the end. Today, credit control rests largely with the central bank and treasury in each country. But even central banks and national treasuries cannot still have the cake they eat; they can't slow down credit expansion and at the same time keep money excessively cheap for governmental borrowing. When a Federal Reserve Bank buys government bonds to peg the price, Federal Reserve money flows out and increases the very money supply which the Federal Reserve is trying in other ways to reduce.

If the great, damaging swings of business cycles are to be avoided, money rates must be allowed a natural response to over-extension of credit. This does not necessarily call for drastic changes in interest rates. Chapter 4 has made plain that again and again when the step has been taken in time, moderate rate adjustments have been enough. But there is always the possibility of inflationary conditions which might demand sizable changes. Hence, rates should be flexible enough to enable credit control to play its part either in curbing inflation or resisting deflation.

It is no secret that the Treasury and the Federal Reserve System have differed over how fast and how far to get away from wartime easy money. The Treasury has been unwilling to go as rapidly in this direction as the Federal Reserve, with its responsibility for credit control, has wished. The Treasury has a commendable desire to keep interest rates low, but when inflation threatens it is a wiser policy to subordinate minor savings in interest to the maintenance of sound credit conditions.

During the past year or so, the Treasury and Federal Reserve have taken an encouraging succession of steps away from frozen low interest rates, as described in Chapter 4. Looking ahead, we should move toward less and less interference with the free movement of interest rates—to greater flexibility so that interest may perform its proper economic function.

5. NOURISH A DYNAMIC ECONOMY

After each great war, the national debt seemed at the time almost unbearable. In some countries and at some times the fear was justified; the currency collapsed. Britain and the United States in the past have borne their debts well. The chief reason is clear: the force of enterprise was so powerful and production and incomes grew so rapidly that there were ample means to pay debt charges.

This process is referred to in Chapter 2 as "growing up to the debt." The phrase is vividly illustrated by a famous pas-

sage in Lord Macaulay's *History of England* published in
1855. There the historian describes the gloomy forebodings
with which many Englishmen viewed the growth of the
national debt during the century before and including the
Napoleonic wars, and how and why these pessimistic predic-
tions failed:

> "At every stage in the growth of that debt it has been
> seriously asserted by wise men that bankruptcy and ruin
> were at hand. Yet still the debt went on growing; and
> still bankruptcy and ruin were as remote as ever. . . .
> . . . "While shallow politicians were repeating that
> the energies of the people were borne down by the
> weight of the public burdens, the first journey was per-
> formed by steam on a railway. Soon the island was in-
> tersected by railways. A sum exceeding the whole
> amount of the national debt at the end of the American
> war was, in a few years, voluntarily expended by this
> ruined people in viaducts, tunnels, embankments,
> bridges, stations, engines. Meanwhile, taxation was
> almost constantly becoming lighter and lighter; yet still
> the Exchequer was full. It may now [1855] be affirmed
> without fear of contradiction that we find it as easy to
> pay the interest of eight hundred millions as our an-
> cestors found it, a century ago, to pay the interest of
> eighty millions. . . .
> "Here it is sufficient to say that the prophets of evil
> were under a double delusion. They erroneously imag-
> ined that there was an exact analogy between the case
> of an individual who is in debt to another individual
> and the case of a society which is in debt to a part of
> itself. . . . They were under an error no less serious
> touching the resources of the country. They made no
> allowance for the effect produced by the incessant prog-

ress of every experimental science, and by the incessant efforts of every man to get on in life. They saw that the debt grew; and they forgot that other things grew as well as the debt."

Our national debt is greater in size and proportion than any in history, and we must summon all our energy and ingenuity to handle it. This country has an enormous potential. Our heritage and tradition of private enterprise developed powers of productivity never known before. Our best hope to meet our gigantic public debt is by release and stimulation of these resources.

It needs no clairvoyance to see that one of the greatest obstacles to productivity in the United States is the present tax system. It penalizes extra effort and removes incentive for going the extra mile. In wartime, high tax rates could not be avoided; in peacetime they are destructive and repressive and should be reduced, as rapidly as is consistent with sound fiscal policy. The method of reduction should be such that those among us who have the energy, determination and ability to forge ahead be encouraged to make the effort. This means particularly the lowering of individual surtaxes. The 1948 Revenue Act made a good beginning in loosening these tax brakes on incentive, but we must have constantly in mind the need for going further.

There is an apparent but not actual contradiction in calling for tax reduction when debt reduction is so essential. Taxes must be reduced gradually and timed with swings of business, prices, and the budget. This means keeping government expenses down, for tax reduction at the expense of an unbalanced budget and inadequate debt retirement would be folly. But it must be remembered that ultimate reduction of the public debt depends on this nation's dynamic growth. If over a period tax reductions renew incentive and restimulate enterprise, they will pay for themselves many times over.

There are, of course, other brakes on enterprise that need attention, but the tax brake is probably the most powerful. Admittedly, in the inflation of the present time, the tax handicaps to adventure and expansion are not to be seen clearly, but they are there nonetheless and their baneful influence will become more and more apparent as the inflation fever subsides.

SUMMARY

These, then, are essentials in management of our national debt:

1. We must exercise careful watch over the budget. A budget deficit creates debt, and a budget surplus makes debt reduction possible. Therefore, the Number One task of debt management is to control the huge overall total of government spending. This is partly a problem of improving the quality of government, by more effective administration and by attracting and holding able people in public service. It is partly a question of our philosophy of government—of what to expect from the central government and what should be left to local government and to individual initiative and self-reliance.

2. We must plan a debt reduction policy which is related to the state of business activity of the country. A heavy retirement of debt in time of prosperity would tend to check over-expansion and inflationary tendencies, while less retirement in times of adversity would relieve the burden of taxation and aid recovery. A reasonable tentative program is to agree now on an annual amount that seems feasible in relation to national income, and if necessary adjust it later.

3. We must distribute the debt as widely as possible among non-bank investors, and so reduce the inflationary money

supply that accompanies a national debt heavily concentrated in the hands of the banking system.

4. We must restore flexibility to interest rates so as to give monetary authorities more freedom in determining credit policies. Rates must have more scope for performing their economic function of adjusting the supply of savings to the demand for investment funds. This will help to discourage extremes of boom and bust.

5. We must take every possible step to preserve and to increase the dynamic energy of our economic life, for it will make the burden of debt easier to bear and will help to maintain our American tradition of freedom. Because high taxes are one of the greatest handicaps to productivity in this country, they should be reduced as rapidly as sound fiscal policy permits. Since such reductions should be tuned to the swings of business, prices, and the budget, this emphasizes the need for cutting expenditures enough so that both debt and tax reduction are possible.

With a program embodying these essentials, the Committee on Public Debt Policy is confident this country can carry its heavy load of debt and still maintain the free and vigorous economy that has been our glory and strength over the years. The task is not easy. It needs courage and wisdom, a high order of statesmanship on the part of our leaders, and understanding and unity among the people.

Though debt management may seem abstract and remote to the average person, it is actually a job in which everyone can—indeed must inevitably—play a part. It involves decisions in such matters as interest rates, taxes, the amounts and purposes of government spending—which affect all of us indirectly and most of us directly. Each question is a test of how clearly we see the issues, whether we act as citizens rather than think primarily of selfish interests. The sum-total of such reactions determines public opinion and shapes public policy.

Happily, the country is endowed with rich gifts—an intelligent citizenry, great wealth in natural resources, boundless opportunities for development, and a tradition of venturing and energetic enterprise which has constantly pressed forward the frontiers of accomplishment. If we have wisdom to cherish these priceless advantages, which have brought us so far already, we should meet and surmount this challenge as we have met and surmounted greater crises in the past.

APPENDIX

APPENDIX

TABLE 10

UNITED STATES GOVERNMENT BUDGET RE-
CEIPTS, EXPENDITURES, AND PUBLIC DEBT, 1914-
1950

(Amounts in millions)

Year Ended June 30	Total Net Receipts	Total Net Expend-itures	Net Sur-plus or Deficit (—)	Public Debt June 30
1914	$ 735	$ 735	$ 0	$ 1,188
1915	698	761	— 63	1,191
1916	782	734	48	1,225
1917	1,124	1,977	— 853	2,976
1918	3,664	12,697	— 9,033	12,244
1919	5,152	18,515	—13,363	25,482
1920	6,695	6,403	292	24,299
1921	5,625	5,116	509	23,977
1922	4,109	3,373	736	22,963
1923	4,007	3,295	712	22,350
1924	4,012	3,049	963	21,251
1925	3,780	3,063	717	20,516
1926	3,963	3,098	865	19,643
1927	4,129	2,974	1,155	18,512
1928	4,042	3,103	939	17,604
1929	4,033	3,299	734	16,931
1930	4,178	3,440	738	16,185
1931	3,190	3,652	— 462	16,801
1932	2,006	4,535	— 2,529	19,487
1933	2,080	3,864	— 1,784	22,539
1934	3,116	6,011	— 2,895	27,053
1935	3,800	7,010	— 3,210	28,701

For footnotes, see end of table.

TABLE 10 (*Continued*)

(Amounts in millions)

Year Ended June 30	Total Net Receipts	Total Net Expenditures	Net Surplus or Deficit (—)	Public Debt June 30
1936	$ 4,116	$ 8,666	$— 4,550	$ 33,779
1937	5,029	8,177	— 3,148	36,425
1938	5,855	7,239	— 1,384	37,165
1939 *	5,097	8,959	— 3,862	40,440
1940	5,296	9,206	— 3,910	42,968
1941	7,227	13,387	— 6,159	48,961
1942	12,696	34,187	—21,490	72,422
1943	22,201	79,622	—57,420	136,696
1944	43,892	95,315	—51,423	201,003
1945	44,762	98,703	—53,941	258,682
1946	40,027	60,703	—20,676	269,422
1947	40,043	39,289	754	258,376
1948	42,211	33,791 ‡	8,419 ‡	252,366
1949 †	39,580	40,180 ‡	— 600 ‡	251,600
1950 †	40,985	41,858	— 873	......

* Figures since 1939 revised to exclude tax refunds from receipts and expenditures.

† January, 1949, estimates.

‡ Does not allow for $3,000,000,000 directed by Congress to be transferred from the 1949 budget to the Foreign Economic Cooperation Trust Fund and charged against 1948, even though actually spent in 1949.

TABLE **II**

GROSS NATIONAL INCOME AND GROSS SAVINGS, 1869-1947,* EXPRESSED IN TERMS OF 1929 DOLLAR VALUES

(Dollar amounts in billions)

	Gross National Income	Gross National Savings	Savings as Per Cent of Income
1869-1878	$ 10.3	$ 2.3	22.3
1874-1883	14.8	3.2	21.6
1879-1888	19.5	4.2	21.5
1884-1893	23.1	5.5	23.8
1889-1898	26.7	6.5	24.3
1894-1903	32.9	7.6	23.1
1899-1908	41.2	8.9	21.6
1904-1913	49.8	10.7	21.5
1909-1918	56.5	12.6	22.3
1919	66.4	16.3	24.5
1920	67.8	15.6	23.0
1921	64.2	10.4	16.2
1922	68.9	12.4	18.0
1923	78.8	16.9	21.4
1924	80.3	14.2	17.7
1925	82.9	18.0	21.7
1926	88.5	18.6	21.0
1927	89.5	17.8	19.9
1928	90.6	17.4	19.2
1929	103.8	15.5	15.0
1930	100.2	12.3	12.3
1931	99.1	10.9	11.0
1932	85.8	4.1	4.7
1933	80.6	3.9	4.9
1934	82.5	7.1	8.6

For footnotes, see end of table.

170

TABLE II (*Continued*)

(Dollar amounts in billions)

	Gross National Income	Gross National Savings	Savings as Per Cent of Income
1935	86.0	9.5	11.0
1936	97.3	13.1	13.5
1937	99.6	11.9	12.0
1938	102.6	10.8	10.5
1939	111.8	14.5	13.0
1940	121.8	18.2	15.0
1941	136.8	23.8	17.4
1942	153.9	38.8	25.2
1943	178.0	43.0	24.2
1944	194.4	51.1	26.3
1945	192.3	41.8	21.7
1946	164.6	21.1	12.8
1947	145.1	15.6	10.8

* The figures from 1869 to 1918 are averages per year by decades.
Sources: 1869-1928, Simon Kuznets, National Product Since 1869 (National Bureau of Economic Research, 1946), p. 52, table I 15 and p. 119, table II 16; 1929-1943, National Income, Supplement to Survey of Current Business, July, 1947 (United States Department of Commerce), 1944-1947, Survey of Current Business, July, 1948.

TABLE I2

ACCUMULATION OF INDIVIDUAL LONG-TERM SAVINGS IN SELECTED INSTITUTIONS, 1920-1947

(Amounts in millions)

Dec. 31	Savings and Loan Associations [1]	Life Insurance Companies [2]	Mutual Savings Banks [3]	Commercial Banks [4]	Postal Savings [5]	Total	Net Increase During Year
1920	$1,741	$5,488	$4,806	$10,546	$ 166	$22,747	....
1921	1,965	5,893	5,541	11,079	148	24,626	$ 1,879
1922	2,210	6,360	5,985	12,289	135	26,979	2,353
1923	2,626	6,981	6,484	13,656	135	29,882	2,903
1924	3,153	7,706	6,912	15,044	137	32,952	3,070
1925	3,811	8,592	7,349	16,314	138	36,204	3,252
1926	4,378	9,594	7,799	17,237	143	39,151	2,947
1927	5,027	10,648	8,352	18,674	153	42,854	3,703
1928	5,762	11,782	8,731	19,295	158	45,728	2,874
1929	6,237	12,801	8,797	19,165	169	47,169	1,441
1930	6,296	13,690	9,384	18,647	250	48,267	1,098
1931	5,916	14,293	9,939	15,955	613	46,716	—1,551
1932	5,326	14,319	9,890	12,101	915	42,551	—4,165
1933	4,750	14,613	9,506	10,979	1,229	41,077	—1,474
1934	4,458	15,687	9,670	11,992	1,232	44,039	2,962
1935	4,254	17,203	9,829	12,899	1,229	45,414	1,375
1936	4,131	18,736	10,013	13,709	1,291	47,880	2,266

1937	4,015	20,181	10,126	14,410	1,303	50,035	2,155
1938	4,005	21,512	10,235	14,427	1,286	51,465	1,430
1939	4,060	23,024	10,481	14,865	1,315	53,745	2,280
1940	4,272	24,663	10,618	15,403	1,342	56,298	2,553
1941	4,652	26,592	10,490	15,523	1,392	58,649	2,351
1942	4,910	28,734	10,621	16,056	1,459	61,780	3,131
1943	5,494	31,365	11,707	19,001	1,837	69,404	7,624
1944	6,305	34,212	13,332	23,871	2,406	80,126	10,722
1945	7,365	37,509	15,332	29,929	3,031	93,148	13,022
1946	8,548	40,713	16,813	33,447	3,379	102,900	9,732
1947 p	9,700	44,000	17,800	35,000	3,500	110,000	7,100

[1] Estimated private investments, excluding pledged shares.

[2] Estimated reserves and dividends left to accumulate, less premium notes and policy loans.

[3] Deposits.

[4] Time deposits.

[5] Outstanding principal and accrued interest on certificates of deposit, outstanding savings stamps and unclaimed deposits.

p Preliminary estimates.

Sources: Home Loan Bank Board, The Spectator, Mutual Savings Banking, Comptroller of the currency, and Post Office Department.

INDEX

175